Kaplan Publishing are constantly finding new ways to make a difference to ~~~~~~~~ and our exciting online resour~~~~~~~~ ~~~mething different to students l~~~~~~~~ ~~ss.

This book comes with fre~~~~~~~~~~~~ resources so that you can study anytime, anywhere.

Having purchased this book, you have access to the following online study materials:

CONTENT	ACCA (including FFA,FAB,FMA)		AAT		FIA (excluding FFA,FAB,FMA)	
	Text	Kit	Text	Kit	Text	Kit
iPaper version of the book	✓	✓	✓	✓	✓	✓
Interactive electronic version of the book	✓					
Fixed tests / progress tests with instant answers	✓		✓			
Mock assessments online			✓	✓		
Material updates	✓	✓	✓	✓	✓	✓
Latest official ACCA exam questions		✓				
Extra question assistance using the signpost icon*		✓				
Timed questions with an online tutor debrief using the clock icon*		✓				
Interim assessment including questions and answers		✓			✓	
Technical articles	✓	✓			✓	✓

* Excludes F1, F2, F3, FFA, FAB, FMA

How to access your online resources

Kaplan Financial students will already have a Kaplan EN-gage account and these extra resources will be available to you online. You do not need to register again, as this process was completed when you enrolled. If you are having problems accessing online materials, please ask your course administrator.

If you are already a registered Kaplan EN-gage user go to www.EN-gage.co.uk and log in. Select the 'add a book' feature and enter the ISBN number of this book and the unique pass key at the bottom of this card. Then click 'finished' or 'add another book'. You may add as many books as you have purchased from this screen.

If you purchased through Kaplan Flexible Learning or via the Kaplan Publishing website you will automatically receive an e-mail invitation to Kaplan EN·gage online. Please register your details using this email to gain access to your content. If you do not receive the e-mail or book content, please contact Kaplan Flexible Learning.

If you are a new Kaplan EN-gage user register at www.EN-gage.co.uk and click on the link contained in the email we sent you to activate your account. Then select the 'add a book' feature, enter the ISBN number of this book and the unique pass key at the bottom of this card. Then click 'finished' or 'add another book'.

Your Code and Information

This code can only be used once for the registration of one book online. This registration and your online content will expire when the final sittings for the examinations covered by this book have taken place. Please allow one hour from the time you submit your book details for us to process your request.

Please scratch the film to access your EN-gage code.

DRFS-nUO2-v2fY-pgMW

Please be aware that this code is case-sensitive and you will need to include the dashes within the passcode, but not when entering the ISBN. For further technical support, please visit www.EN-gage.co.uk

COMPUTERISED ACCOUNTING

Qualifications and Credit Framework

Level 2 Certificate in Accounting

British Library Cataloguing-in-Publication Data

A catalogue record for this book is available from the British Library.

Published by
Kaplan Publishing UK
Unit 2, The Business Centre
Molly Millars Lane
Wokingham
Berkshire
RG41 2QZ

ISBN 978-0-85732-594-5

Printed and bound in Great Britain.

We are grateful to the Association of Accounting Technicians for permission to reproduce past assessment materials and example tasks based on the new syllabus. The solutions to past answers and similar activities in the style of the new syllabus have been prepared by Kaplan Publishing.

We are grateful to HM Revenue and Customs for the provision of tax forms, which are Crown Copyright and are reproduced here with kind permission from the Office of Public Sector Information.

CONTENTS

STUDY TEXT AND WORKBOOK

INTRODUCTION

HOW TO USE THESE MATERIALS

These Kaplan Publishing learning materials have been carefully designed to make your learning experience as easy as possible and to give you the best chance of success in your AAT assessments.

They contain a number of features to help you in the study process.

The sections on the Unit Guide, the Assessment and Study Skills should be read before you commence your studies.

They are designed to familiarise you with the nature and content of the assessment and to give you tips on how best to approach your studies.

STUDY TEXT

This study text has been specially prepared for the revised AAT qualification introduced in July 2010.

It uses a case study approach to guide you through the syllabus and builds up your knowledge and skills chapter by chapter. The text is based upon Sage Instant Account V16, but can also be followed if you are using Sage Line 50 or other versions of Sage Instant Accounts.

UNIT GUIDE

Computerised Accounting consists of one unit.

Unit
3 credits

Purpose of the units

The AAT has stated that the general purpose of this unit is about using a computerised accounting application to:

Input and process data for business transactions including sales and purchases, receipts and payments, and prepare management and period end reports.

Learning outcomes

On completion of this unit the learner will be able to:

- Access, enter and edit accounting information.
- Select and use tools and techniques to process business transactions.
- Produce accounting documents and summary reports to meet requirements.

Knowledge

To perform this unit effectively you will need to know and understand the following:

		Chapter
1	**Access, enter and edit accounting information**	
1.1	Describe the sources and characteristics of accounting data	1
1.2	Set up and create new accounting data records accurately to meet requirements	3, 5, 6, 7
1.3	Locate and display accounting data records to meet requirements	3, 5, 6, 7
1.4	Check data records meet needs using IT tools, making corrections as necessary	4
1.5	Respond appropriately to data entry error messages	4
1.6	Describe the risks to data security and procedures used for data protection	1
1.7	Apply local and/or legal guidelines for the storage and use of data	1
2	**Select and use tools and techniques to process business transactions**	
2.1	Select and use appropriate tools and techniques to enter and process transactions	8, 9
2.2	Review transaction process and indentify any errors	8, 9, 10, 12
2.3	Respond appropriately to any transactions errors and problems	8, 9, 10, 12
2.4	Select and use appropriate tools and techniques to process period end routines	8, 9, 10

Chapter

Delivery guidance

The AAT have provided delivery guidance giving further details of the way in which the unit will be assessed.

Learners must be able to take and print screen shots of their work and be able to refer to the help guidelines included in the software package.

Access, enter and edit accounting information

1.1 Learners need to understand what source documentation is used to enter data on to the computer. They must also be able to understand why coding is needed within the accounting system and how to allocate codes to customers' and suppliers' accounts. Students also need to understand the legal requirements for document retention.

1.2, 1.3 Learners should be able to set the software system date, i.e. today's date, as required. They should set up, use and amend records and ledger accounts for new and existing credit customers and credit suppliers, using data entry instructions or the appropriate software tool (the wizard). This includes entering credit control details, opening balances, brought forward and/or nil opening balances.

Learners should be able to set up and use general ledger accounts, using data entry instructions or the appropriate software tool. This includes:

- Select accounts from the default list of accounts provided by the software

- Amending the account names used in the default list of accounts provided by the software, for example change 'ordinary share capital' to 'capital'

- Adding new accounts to the default list of accounts provided by the software

- Entering opening balances
- Checking opening entries using the trial balance

1.4, 1.5 Learners need to check their own work for accuracy at all times and use appropriate software tools to verify data is correct. Make corrections within limits of responsibility, or follow organisational procedures for reporting errors and problems.

1.6, 1.7 Students need to understand:

- The risks to data such as loss and/or theft, illegal copying, poor storage, viruses, unauthorised access in confidential information, and
- The possible consequences of these risks, and
- Ways to reduce these risks such as use of passwords, how to choose a password in accordance with best practice, back up of data, the use of appropriate file names, proper storage of data including back up copies and virus protection

Learners need to be aware of the basic requirements of the Data Protection Act and relevant organisational policy in relation to security and back up procedures. The back up of data to a suitable storage device at regular intervals.

Select and use tools and techniques to process business transactions

2.1, 2.2, 2.3, 2.4

Learners need to be able to process transactions involving different rates of VAT. The rate of VAT will always be given:

- Standard rated
- Zero rate VAT
- VAT not applicable

Post entries to record sales and purchase invoices and credit notes, in batches or singly, using if necessary, general ledger accounts not previously set up.

Post payments received from credit customers and payments made to credit suppliers. Payments in this instance can compromise cash, cheques, automated payments and set off payments (contra entries). Settlement discounts may apply.

Learners must be able to post entries to record:

- Cash purchases and sales – payments made/received by cash, cheque or debit card, but NOT credit card

- Sundry income received by cash or cheque
- Payments for items other than the purchase of goods, made by cash, cheque or debit card, but NOT credit card
- Petty cash transactions including re-imbursements of petty cash float
- Standing orders and direct debits
- Transfers between bank accounts
- Bad debts written off
- Bank interest paid and received

Learners must post journal entries, or use an appropriate tool in the software package where relevant to:

- Amend opening balances
- Remove duplicate entries
- Correct given and own errors

Process period end routines:

- Extract a trial balance. Trace and correct own errors
- Update the bank account where necessary from a bank statement and prepare a bank reconciliation statement. If the bank reconciliation statement does not agree trace and correct own errors
- Clear month end turnover totals

Produce accounting documents and summary reports to meet requirements

3.1, 3.2, 3.3

Learners must understand who requires accounting data and in what form it is required. Data includes details of customers and suppliers, ledger balances, bank reconciliation statement, audit trail, aged debtor/creditor analysis, statement of account, monthly sales figures.

Prepare and print:

- Customer and supplier lists
- Sales, purchases and returns day books
- Sales ledger accounts, or specific accounts only
- Purchases ledger accounts, or specific accounts only
- General ledger accounts, or specific accounts only
- Petty cash and all bank accounts, or specific accounts only

- The journal
- A trial balance
- Bank reconciliation statement
- Audit trail
- Aged debtor/creditor analysis
- Statements of account to be sent to credit customers
- Letters to customers re overdue accounts

3.4 Learners must be able to import and export data and link to other systems and software. Process simple data export tasks to other systems and software such as:

- Export a customer statement for email
- Export aged debtor/creditor analysis to a spreadsheet
- Screen shots

Be aware of and able to answer questions on:

- All types of data that can be exported to other systems and software
- Types of data that can be imported from other systems and software and in what format

Learners will NOT be required to

- Set up company details or the accounting year
- Generate profit and loss accounts and balance sheets
- Post depreciation or accruals and prepayments
- Prepare or update budgets
- Prepare invoices or credit notes
- Create or use product/stock records

THE ASSESSMENT

The format of the assessment

The purpose of the assessment is to allow the learner to demonstrate the skills and knowledge necessary to use computerised accounting software at level 2.

The assessment is designed to allow the use of any accounting software package and is the form of a project initially. In the short term it is likely to be your local tuition provider who assess your work, although the AAT do hope to introduce a computer based test with immediate results in the near future.

Work based evidence can also be submitted for this unit and would be assessed by your local tuition provider.

Part 1. This consists of an assignment asking the learner to input data into a computerised accounting package and produce documents and reports. This can be completed over a period of four sessions to replicate the workflow in an office environment.

Part 2. Contains several short written tasks which must be completed in one session

Section 2 covers:

- Develop skills and knowledge to meet personal and organisational needs

Learners will be required to complete tasks, based upon a case study, some of which may require further research by the learner. The learner's completed answers to the set tasks will be presented for assessment in the form of a file as part of this unit is about communication, literacy and numeracy skills. The presentation of the finished work is extremely important and will be assessed as well as the content of the answers.

The assessment material will normally be provided by the AAT, delivered online and assessed locally. Learners will be required to demonstrate competence in both sections of the assessment.

Alternatively, with guidance and support from training providers learners can provide workplace evidence to be assessed locally by their training provider. The training provider will be required to ensure that all assessment criteria are covered.

STUDY SKILLS

Preparing to study

Devise a study plan

Determine which times of the week you will study.

Split these times into sessions of at least one hour for study of new material. Any shorter periods could be used for revision or practice.

Put the times you plan to study onto a study plan for the weeks from now until the assessment and set yourself targets for each period of study – in your sessions make sure you cover the whole course, activities and the associated questions in the workbook at the back of the manual.

If you are studying more than one unit at a time, try to vary your subjects as this can help to keep you interested and see subjects as part of wider knowledge.

When working through your course, compare your progress with your plan and, if necessary, re-plan your work (perhaps including extra sessions) or, if you are ahead, do some extra revision / practice questions.

Effective studying

Active reading

You are not expected to learn the text by rote, rather, you must understand what you are reading and be able to use it to pass the assessment and develop good practice.

A good technique is to use SQ3Rs – Survey, Question, Read, Recall, Review:

1 Survey the chapter

Look at the headings and read the introduction, knowledge, skills and content, so as to get an overview of what the chapter deals with.

2 Question

Whilst undertaking the survey ask yourself the questions you hope the chapter will answer for you.

3   Read

Read through the chapter thoroughly working through the activities and, at the end, making sure that you can meet the learning objectives highlighted on the first page.

4   Recall

At the end of each section and at the end of the chapter, try to recall the main ideas of the section / chapter without referring to the text. This is best done after short break of a couple of minutes after the reading stage.

5   Review

Check that your recall notes are correct.

You may also find it helpful to re-read the chapter to try and see the topic(s) it deals with as a whole.

Note taking

Taking notes is a useful way of learning, but do not simply copy out the text.

The notes must:

- be in your own words
- be concise
- cover the key points
- well organised
- be modified as you study further chapters in this text or in related ones.

Trying to summarise a chapter without referring to the text can be a useful way of determining which areas you know and which you don't.

Three ways of taking notes

1   Summarise the key points of a chapter

2   Make linear notes

A list of headings, subdivided with sub-headings listing the key points.

If you use linear notes, you can use different colours to highlight key points and keep topic areas together.

Use plenty of space to make your notes easy to use.

3 Try a diagrammatic form

The most common of which is a mind map.

To make a mind map, put the main heading in the centre of the paper and put a circle around it.]

Draw lines radiating from this to the main sub-headings which again have circles around them.

Continue the process from the sub-headings to sub-sub-headings.

Highlighting and underlining

You may find it useful to underline or highlight key points in your study text – but do be selective.

You may also wish to make notes in the margins.

Further reading

In addition to this text, you should also read the "Student section" of the "Accounting Technician" magazine every month to keep abreast of any guidance from the examiners.

An introduction to computerised accounting

Introduction

The aim of this manual is to guide you through the computerised accounting aspects of your studies.

To complete this manual you will need an understanding of the basics of double entry bookkeeping and a copy of SAGE. There are a number of versions of SAGE; this manual uses SAGE Instant Accounts version 15. If you have another version of SAGE, or even another accounting package, you should still be able to proceed without too much difficulty, although you may find that some of the screen-shots used in the manual differ.

The manual uses a case study approach to guide you step-by-step. It assumes that you have never used a computerised accounting package before. Even if you have, it is worth starting at the beginning to ensure that you don't 'jump ahead' too quickly.

KNOWLEDGE	CONTENTS
1.1 Describe the sources and characteristics of accounting data	1 Manual and computerised bookkeeping
1.6 Describe the risks to data security and procedures used for data protection	2 Benefits of a computerised system
1.7 Apply local and/or legal guidelines for the storage and use of data	3 Accounting documents
	4 Retention of documents
	5 Coding
	6 Risks of using a computerised system

1 Manual and computerised bookkeeping

The double entry system of bookkeeping that is still used today was developed in Italy in the fifteenth century. With the introduction of affordable and reliable information technology in the last thirty years, it was perhaps inevitable that business organisations would look to find ways to computerise their bookkeeping systems. Now it is rare to find an organisation which does not use some form of computer to aid in the day-to-day record keeping that is an essential aspect to running a business, whether large or small.

For very small organisations, a simple spreadsheet to record monies in and out of the business may suffice. However, once a business becomes larger or more complex, it may be beneficial to introduce a computerised bookkeeping system. There are many proprietary versions on the market, each of which works in a similar way but which will offer different approaches to data entry, presentation of reports and so on, as well as different 'extras' such as stock management modules, budgeting and tax planning. Some systems also allow a company to integrate a computerised payroll function.

2 Benefits of a computerised system

The main benefits ascribed to a computerised bookkeeping system are:

- Quicker, more efficient processing of data

- Fewer mathematical errors – because the system completes all the double entry and other mathematical functions (e.g. calculation of percentages) there is reduced opportunity for human error

- Accounting documents (e.g. invoices, statements etc) can be generated automatically, using tailored documents designed to incorporate company details, logos etc

- The range of information that can be easily produced in reports is wide and varied, meaning businesses can report to various internal and external groups (e.g. management, directors, shareholders, banks etc) in an appropriate format

- There is no need for manual processing of data – computerised bookkeeping systems complete all the double entry automatically

- Hardware and software prices have fallen dramatically over the last thirty years, making a computerised system affordable to all organisations

- Allow data to be easily transferred into other programs – e.g. a spreadsheet or word processing package

3 Accounting documents

Business organizations rely on relevant documentation to record the transactions that it undertakes. Without an appropriate piece of supporting documentation, there is no way of knowing what has been bought, from whom and for how much, nor indeed what has been sold. With a high proportion of modern transactions being on credit, an accurate and comprehensive system of recording transactions is essential.

Many business documents are referred to as 'Primary Records'. They include:

- purchase orders
- delivery notes
- purchase invoices
- debit notes
- credit notes
- sales invoices
- debit notes

These documents are used to record business transactions in the first instance. For example, if an organisation wishes to purchase a new computer printer, it may first raise a purchase order which is sent to the supplier. The supplier would issue or deliver the printer along with a delivery note, to record the safe receipt of the goods. A supplier invoice requiring payment would follow. If the printer was faulty, it could be returned and a credit note issued.

In order for a transaction to be correctly recorded in a computerised accounting system, the appropriate documentation must first be raised and then the details entered into 'the system'; indeed, many organisations employ accounting staff whose job is primarily to enter the data accurately and completely from the source documents.

There are many other documents which are also essential in maintaining an up-to-date and accurate accounting system. Bank statements, schedules of direct debits/standing orders, supplier statements, correspondence from suppliers and customers and so on also provide invaluable information which can be used to check the computerised bookkeeping system for accuracy.

In the course of the case study which follows, you will be required to enter details from a range of source documents, and use other documents, to maintain a computerised bookkeeping system for a small company.

4 Retention of documents

There are legal requirements for businesses to retain source documents beyond the end of the accounting period to which they relate. The Limitations Act 1980 deals with this issue in general; however, there are many other pieces of specific legislation which place a responsibility on businesses to retain their records.

Accounting and Banking Records	
Ledgers, invoices, cheques, paying-in documents, bank statements and standing order instructions	Must all be retained for a minimum of six years
Employee Records	
All personnel records	6 years from end of employment
Senior Executive personnel records	Permanently
Rejected job applications	One year
Time cards, payroll records and expenses claims	Six years
Medical records and accident records	Permanently
Contractual Arrangements	
Simple contracts – e.g. with suppliers or customers	6 years after expiration of contract
Contracts relating to land and buildings	12 years after expiration of contract
Trust deeds (e.g. mortgages)	Permanently

Statutory Returns and Records of Board Meetings	
All statutory returns (e.g. to Companies House)	Permanently
Notices, circulars and minutes of board meetings	Permanently

Safe retention of records such as these is important not only to fulfil an organisation's legal obligations, but also because they may prove an invaluable source of reference – for example in a future complaint against a supplier.

However, all organisations must ensure that these documents are stored in such a way that they are easily accessible if required, kept secure from unauthorised access, and kept safe from physical damage (e.g. water or fire damage).

5 Coding

All computerised bookkeeping systems work by the use of codes. Each supplier and each customer must be given a unique code by which the computer software can recognise them. It is vital that there can be no confusion between two suppliers with similar names. For example, you may be fully aware that John Green and John Greenwood are entirely different people, but it could be easy for a computer to mix them up. Each must therefore be given a unique code by which they can be identified.

Similarly, each product manufactured or sold by an organisation may be given a unique code. Employees, also, are usually 'coded' – you could check your pay slip to find your own Employee Reference Number.

Finally, every type of income or expense, asset or liability, is given a unique code to identify it. This makes entering transactions quite straightforward, since you need only refer to the relevant four digit code rather than a long narrative description.

Codes must be unique. However, they should also be recognisable by the person dealing with the system. For example, if a supplier was coded "SMITH006", this would be far more recognisable than a purely numeric code such as "0827329".

Care must be taken to issue codes that are not ambiguous. The use of a combination of letters and numbers (an alphanumeric code) often achieves this.

In SAGE, when you create a new customer or supplier record, the program will automatically suggest a code for that supplier. It does this by taking the first eight characters of the name. The suggested code for a customer called Greenwood would therefore be "GREENWOO". You may decide this is not the most appropriate code (think what the problem might be if you had two different suppliers called Greenwood), in which case you can easily change it. Many organisations have a set structure for coding, and if this is the case in your organisation you should follow it.

6 Risks of using a computerised system

Computerised accounting systems may offer a lot of advantages to businesses, but organisations must also be aware of the potential risks posed by such systems. These risks can be categorised as:

- Physical risks – caused by system failure, theft, damage or loss or corruption of data, and access to systems or data by unauthorised users

- Virus threats – the risk of a computer virus (or similar) being introduced to a network, with the resultant loss of or damage to data

- Legal threats – from contravention of legislation such as the Data Protection Act (1998) by an organisation in the way that it stores or uses personal data.

Accounting data is particularly at risk, because it is highly confidential and potentially highly valuable to other people. Hence you must remain especially vigilant to risks to data security.

Types of Risk

Physical Risks

Risk	Possible Safeguards
Damage from spillage (e.g. liquid)	• No food or drink permitted near computer workstations
Electrical connections becoming worn or damaged	• Keep workstations and desks tidy, with all cabling carefully and tidily arranged • Avoid overloading circuits by plugging too many plugs into a socket or adaptor • Carry out regular visual checks for frayed cables, exposed wires etc. Report any incidences that you find
Theft of computer hardware	• Hardware may be fastened to desks etc (although it may still be possible to open the casing to remove hard drives) • Regular physical checks of IT equipment to ensure the actual equipment matches that held on the Fixed Asset Register • Use of bar-codes and other identifying details to ensure that any items stolen can be quickly returned if found
Damage to, or loss of, memory devices (e.g. disks, USB pen drives)	• Treat all storage devices with care. Although modern devices are quite durable, they can still be scratched or damaged. Even grease left by fingerprints can damage the effectiveness of the disk. • Avoid exposure to devices which contain large magnets – this can corrupt data on the storage device

	• Be extremely vigilant if you are taking memory devices with you out of the office – to work at home or on the train, for example. There are many examples of instances where highly confidential data has been lost in this way. Remember, the data on the disk is usually far more valuable than the device itself • Taking regular backups of data which are named appropriately and stored off-site in secure storage.
'Prying eyes' – unauthorised viewing of confidential information by colleagues, clients or others	• Remember, if you can see confidential information on your computer screen, others may be able to as well. Angle your screen and arrange your workspace to minimise the risk of other people seeing your work. • Always log out of a program if you are leaving your desk • Do not leave confidential papers on your desk. Be especially wary if there are people other than colleagues in your office • Use a password to protect access to your computer, and make sure that the program automatically logs you out after a few minutes of inactivity

Virus Threats

All computers that are linked to 'the outside world' (e.g. via a network or to the internet) are susceptible to security threats. Many people are familiar with the threat posed by viruses or other similar threats.

A virus is a piece of software that is used to maliciously infect your computer. What is more, it then has the ability to replicate itself and infect any other computer that is connected to yours. Of course, this also means that your computer is at risk of being infected by other computers as well.

Introduction of the virus to a system usually takes place when you open a file that has been deliberately infected – for example, an email attachment or a web-site, an infected piece of software, or an infected memory device (e.g. a memory stick).

The consequences of being infected by a virus are many:

- Infecting all other computers you are linked to

- Deleting particular files – especially files which are essential to the normal operation of your computer

- Altering files so they are no longer legible

- Slowing down your computer by taking up huge amounts of memory – leaving your computer extremely slow and unable to perform basic tasks

- Access your data and send it to other people

- 'Read' your passwords for essential sites such as on-line banking – enabling somebody else to access your bank account

- Wiping your hard-drive – essentially deleting everything from the computer.

Safeguards against Viruses

Firewalls: these are designed to prevent 'hackers' gaining access to a computer network via the phone line. These can be a piece of software (now often built in to operating systems such as Windows) or a hardware firewall, which is essentially a box which acts as a barrier between the modem (the phone line into your computer) and the computer itself. An effective firewall is an essential aspect of computer safeguarding, particularly where users have access to the internet.

Effective IT Policies: most organisations now have clearly defined IT policies regarding the private use of the internet and e-mails, not allowing employees to install their own software (e.g. games) on work computers.

Using Virus Protection Software: this is the most important method of protecting computer systems. It acts as a guard dog, constantly watching for suspicious files, blocking or destroying them and advising the user that there has been an attempt to compromise the security of the system. As virus protection programs are constantly being updated with details of new viruses, it is essential that it is kept updated and current at all times. An out-of-date program is no protection against the most recent viruses.

Personal Vigilance: Be very wary if you receive unsolicited emails from addresses that you do not recognise. Do not open any emails that you are suspicious of – you should report these to your IT manager or your supervisor. However, you should also be wary of emails (particularly those with attachments) from addresses you do recognise – remember, if somebody you know has a computer which has been infected there is a high probability that the computer will then try and attack your computer as well.

Be very careful when accessing the internet. Only use sites you need for work. Be wary of links to other sites that you do not recognise. Again, if you are in any doubt, or suspect that your computer may have been the victim of a virus, inform your supervisor.

Passwords

Passwords are one of the most common – and most abused – forms of computer security. In most businesses the access to each computer is protected by a password, as well as access to different pieces of software. Even individual files and documents can and should be protected if they contain confidential or sensitive information.

The choice of password is very important; you should be able to remember it, but it should not be easily guessed by others. Ideally, a password should:

- Be at least 6-8 characters long
- Contain a mixture of upper and lower case letters and numbers
- Not be a recognisable word

Under no circumstances should you choose something like your own name, you child's name or your pet dog's name – these are far too easy for someone with only a small amount of knowledge about you to guess. You should also avoid obvious combinations such as 'password' or '123456'.

You should be able to remember your own password. Do not be tempted to write it down in your diary, on a scrap of paper in your top drawer, or even on a sticky note and attach it to the monitor!

KAPLAN PUBLISHING

You should also never tell anybody else your password – even your most trusted colleague. If you do suspect that somebody knows what your password is, you should change it immediately.

Many systems are configured to require you to change your password every few weeks – even if yours is not, this is good practice.

Back ups

Occasionally data is lost, whether through an unforeseen circumstance such as a fire or through computer failure. It is therefore essential that organisation's take appropriate steps to minimise the risk of data loss, and to minimise the impact of data loss if it does happen.

Backups should be taken on a regular basis, and at least once a day in most businesses. In addition, individual files should regularly be backed up whilst working on them. There is little more frustrating than spending an hour producing a document or a spreadsheet only to lose it and not to have a back up.

Many programs (including Microsoft Office applications) have an auto-recovery function – essentially a back up is taken automatically every few minutes without the user having to do anything. If there is an interruption or failure (e.g. a power cut) only a small amount of work would be lost, and the affected file can very quickly and easily be recovered.

Copies of backups should be kept securely to prevent unauthorised access or accidental damage. It is good practice to keep a back up at a secondary location (i.e. off site). This way, if there is a fire or a burglary the backup data will not be destroyed or stolen. Some businesses may still take physical backups off site (such as a CD), but this increases the risk of that back up being lost or stolen while away from the office. It is becoming increasingly common for organisations to pay an IT company to keep remote backups electronically.

The Data Protection Act (1998)

The Data Protection Act (DPA) is designed to protect the rights of the individual whose personal data is held and used by other people or organisations.

Personal data are defined in the DPA as:

"data which relate to a living individual who can be identified:

- from those data or

- from those data and other information which is in the possession of, or likely to come into the possession of, the *data controller* and includes any expression of opinion about the individual and any indication of the intentions of the data controller or any other person in respect of the individual"

The data controller is a person who determines the purposes for which and the manner in which any personal data are, or are to be, processed.

Example

If you have enrolled at a local college or training provider for your AAT program, you will have been required to complete an enrolment form. The information you will have completed on the enrolment form is likely to have included your name, gender, ethnicity, birthday, address, national insurance number, your qualifications, any health issues you may have, your bank details and so on. It is essential for the college or training provider to have this very personal and confidential information about you to process your application, to secure possible funding and to send you an invoice or set up a direct debit for your course fees.

However, you may then raise the question – what happens to all this information once my application has been processed? How long does the organisation keep the data about me? What else is it used for? Is it sold to any external bodies (e.g. for marketing purposes)?

These questions (and more) are addressed by the Data Protection Act.

The Data Protection Act has EIGHT PRINCIPLES, which state that personal data must be:

1   Processed fairly and lawfully

2   Obtained for specified and lawful purposes

3   Adequate, relevant and not excessive

4   Accurate and up-to-date

5   Not kept any longer than necessary

6   Processed in accordance with the data subject's (i.e. the individual's) rights

7   Securely kept

8   Not transferred to any other country without adequate protection in situ.

Individuals have a number of rights:

- To be informed of all of the information held about them by an organisation

- To prevent the processing of their data for the purposes of direct marketing

- To compensation if they can show that a contravention of the DPA has led to loss or damage

- To have inaccurate data removed or corrected

If the data held by an organisation is *sensitive* then extra safeguards must be put in place. Sensitive data is defined by the act as data pertaining to:

- Racial or ethnic origin
- Religious or similar beliefs
- Trade union membership
- Physical or mental health or sexual life
- Political opinions
- Criminal offences

Data about one or more of these sensitive issues may only be held in strictly defined situations or where explicit consent has been obtained.

Installing SAGE for the first time

CONTENTS

1   Installing SAGE

---

1 Installing SAGE

When you load SAGE v16 for the first time you should see the following screen:

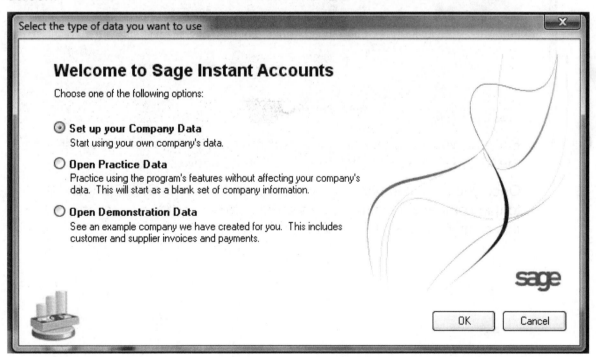

Assuming you are entering a new company (as you will be doing here, make sure that the "set up your company data" is marked. Don't worry at this stage about the other options – just press the ⌐ Next ¬ button.

You should now see this screen:

Your choice here depends on whether you are setting up a new company, or uploading existing data.

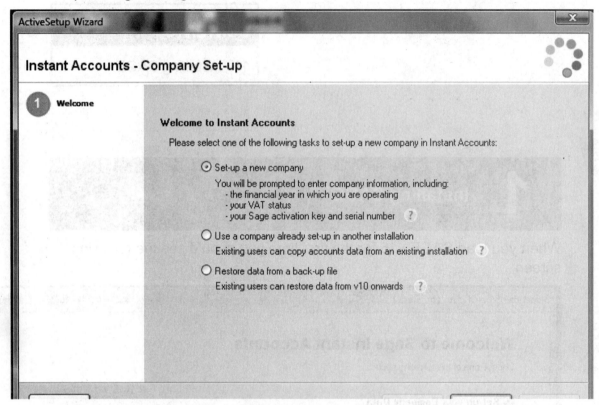

For now, you will be starting with a completely new company, so click on the "SET UP A NEW COMPANY" button as shown.

Once you have company details set up and saved in SAGE, it will default to that company each time you start up. However, it is easy to return to this point if you wish to enter a new company.

Setting up your company

3

KNOWLEDGE

1.2 Set up and create new accounting data records accurately to meet requirements

1.3 Locate and display accounting data records to meet requirements

CONTENTS

1 Background to the company

TotalPhoto Ltd is a small company based in the market town of Miltonby, in Lancashire. It is owned by two directors, Matt Evans and Stuart Lincoln. It was established in 2004 when both Matt and Stuart left Art College. They specialise in contemporary family photography, most of which takes place in their rented studio on a small industrial estate on the outskirts of town. In addition, they also undertake a varied and increasing range of contracted photography, including weddings, dance shows, football competitions etc.

TotalPhoto Ltd has four members of staff, excluding yourself. In addition to Matt and Stuart, there is Sarala, a part-time photographer, and Michelle, the administrator for the company.

Since its inception, the company has used a manual bookkeeping system. However, the company has grown significantly in this time and Matt and Stuart now require more timely financial information on which to manage the company. They have therefore decided to implement a computerised system and to employ you as a part-time bookkeeper for the business.

Today's date is 30th September 2010 – the last day of the company's financial year.

2 Setting up the company

Introduction

When you start using SAGE for your company you must firstly enter some information about the company itself. This is important because it will identify this particular company and appear on various reports. In addition, at this stage, you must enter the dates of the company's financial year. This is vitally important, as SAGE will use this information in producing your annual accounts.

Data

You will need the following information for this session.

Company Name:	TotalPhoto Ltd
Company Address:	Unit 63 Bailey Industrial Estate Fonby Road Miltonby Lancashire LD37 7QZ
Telephone:	01949 969 379
Fax:	01949 969 379
E-mail:	info@totalphotoltd.webnet.uk
Website:	www.totalphotoltd.co.uk
Company Reg. Number:	376 096 82
VAT Number:	734928107
Accounting Period:	1st October – 30th September

Now we can begin entering the data for our company, TotalPhoto Ltd.

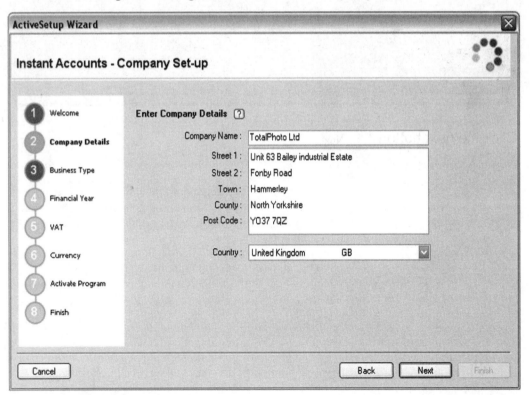

Be sure to check for accuracy – but don't worry if you make a mistake because you can always amend it later. Once you are happy with your entries click on the [Next] button.

Step One – Selecting the business type

On this screen you can choose a business type for your business, this amends the nominal codes so they are specific for your business. For this exercise we are going to the General (standard) type.

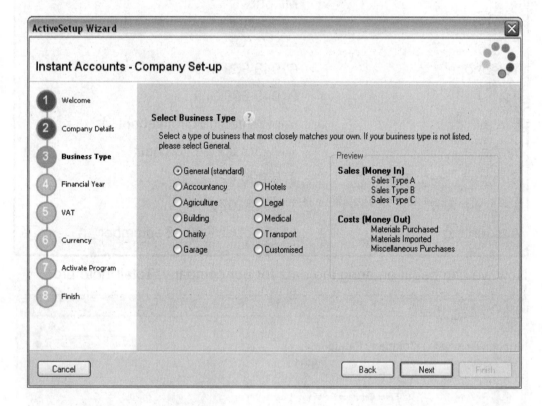

Click the next button [Next]

Step Two – Entering the details of the Financial Year

This is a really important stage. You need to enter the dates of your company's Financial Year. Remember, for TotalPhoto Ltd the company's Financial Year is 1st October to the 30th September.

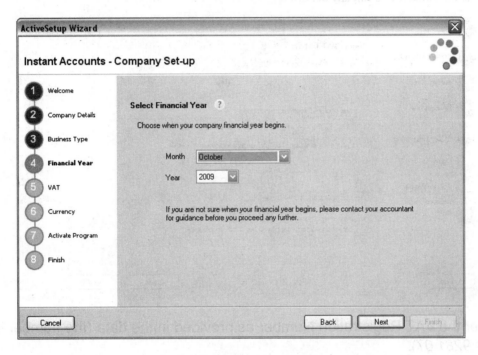

The data in this manual all refers to the year 2009-10, and so our Financial Year will start in **October 2009**. Enter this, using the drop down boxes.

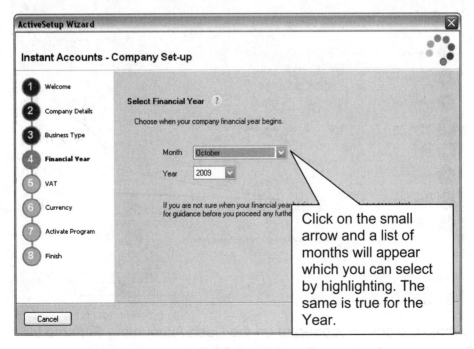

Again, when you have done this press the [Next] button.

Step Three – Entering the VAT Details

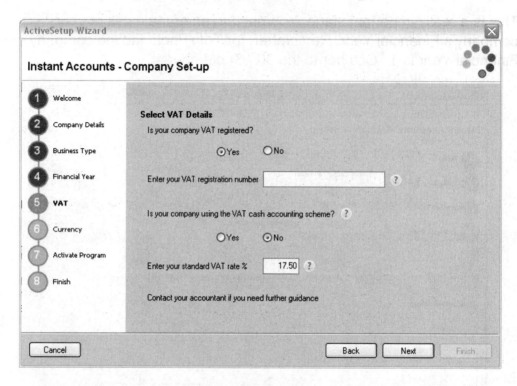

Enter the VAT Registration Number as provided in the data (the number is *734 9281 07*).

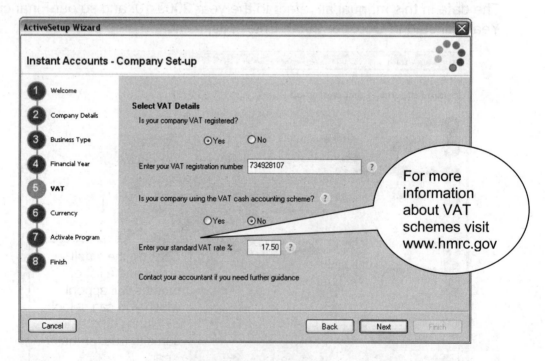

For more information about VAT schemes visit www.hmrc.gov

TotalPhoto Ltd does not operate on the Cash Accounting Scheme for VAT, so you can leave this box empty. Click the Next button.

Step Four – Entering the currency details

At this stage you can enter the currency details. All of TotalPhoto Ltd's transactions take place in the UK, and so their base currency is "Pound Sterling".

You should check that this option is correctly checked.

Again, click the [Next] button to proceed.

Step Five – Activating the SAGE Program

You now need to enter two pieces of information from your SAGE box. You need both the Serial Number and the Activation Key to proceed.

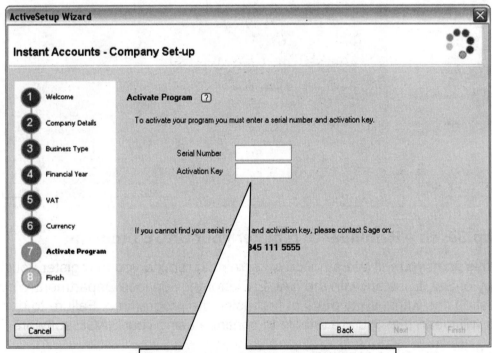

The Serial Number and Activation Key can be found on a sticky label labelled "Important Information" inside your Sage box. These are unique numbers which help to prevent fraudulent use of the software. These are important, and you must keep them in a safe place!

Step Six – Active Setup

Well done – you have now set up SAGE with the basic information needed for the company TotalPhoto Ltd. At this stage you can simply press the

Finish button to move to the next stage.

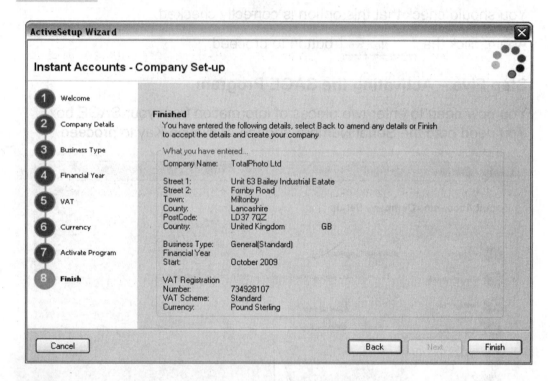

Step Seven – Reminder to register your SAGE program

At this point you will see a notice on screen to remind you to register your copy of SAGE Instant with the SAGE Customer Services Department. You must do this within **sixty days** of first using the programme. Failure to do this will mean that you are unable to continue using your SAGE software.

Click OK to continue.

Navigating SAGE

Introduction

Well Done! You have by now opened your SAGE Instant software and set up the basic details of the company. The next stage is to check your company data and then to practice navigating your way around the different sections of SAGE. Don't worry if you have never used a package like SAGE before – so long as you can use a mouse you will be fine ☺

KNOWLEDGE
1.4 Check data records meet needs using IT tools, making corrections as necessary
1.5 Respond appropriately to data entry error messages.

CONTENTS
1 The opening window – the customer process screen
2 The supplier process screen
3 Checking your company details
4 Dates
5 Checking your data
6 Making corrections
7 Backing up your work

1 The opening window – the customer process screen

This 'window' (or screen) is the one that will now appear every time you open SAGE Instant. You will explore it in more detail as you progress through the manual. For now, just take the time to familiarise yourself with this screen.

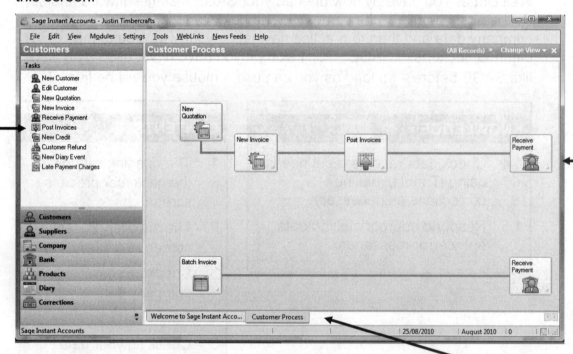

This screen enables you to access a range of accounting activities connected with your customers. You can:

1. Produce a new quotation for a potential customer

2. Create an invoice to send or give to a customer

3. Post (enter) the details of that invoice onto SAGE

4. Produce a statement showing how much a customer owes you

5. Receive and account for a payment made by a customer

Note that you can access each of these activities in a number of ways.

The easiest are via:

a. The *RELATED LINKS TABS* at the bottom of the screen

b. The options on the *TASKS PANEL*

c. The icons on the *CUSTOMER PROCESS* screen

You will practice each of these later on in this manual.

KAPLAN PUBLISHING

Of course, every business needs customers, but they are not the only aspect of a business. Any business will also need suppliers (of goods, raw materials and services). It will then also need to keep a record of the stock that it carries – whether of raw materials, work in progress or finished goods for sale. It will need a bank account (or maybe more than one!) in which to place its receipts and from which to make payments. SAGE also allows you to input accounting activities with each of these.

It is very simple to access the different parts of SAGE.

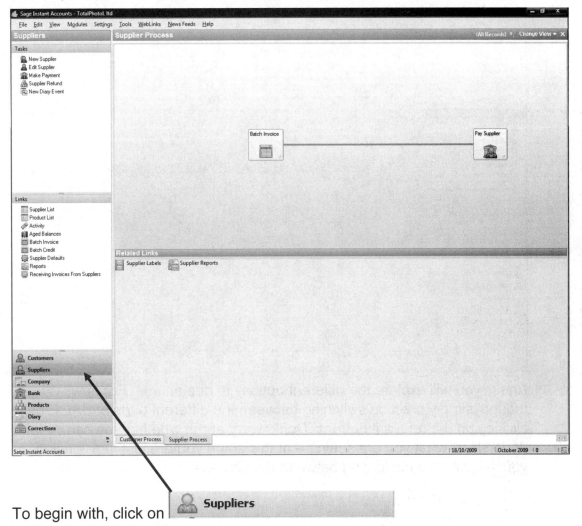

To begin with, click on **Suppliers**

This will bring up a new window with a different series of icons.

2 The supplier process screen

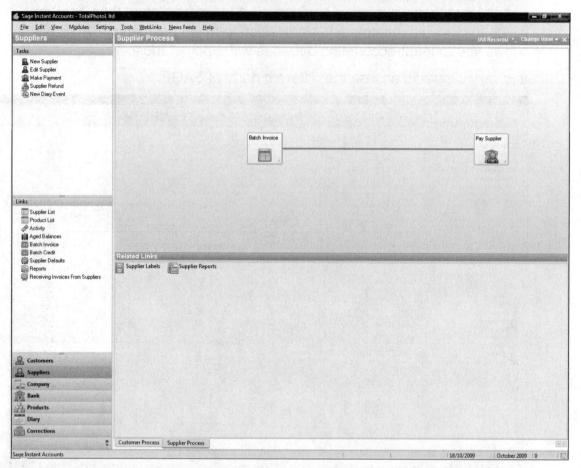

Again, you will explore the different options in due course. For now, though, simply practice switching between the different parts of SAGE by clicking on the relevant buttons. Don't worry about whether you can understand what you are seeing – at this stage you are just familiarising yourself with the navigating between the screens.

KAPLAN PUBLISHING

Exercise

Start at the Customer Process Screen.

Navigate to the following screens:

❶ Suppliers ⇨ Pay Supplier (looks like 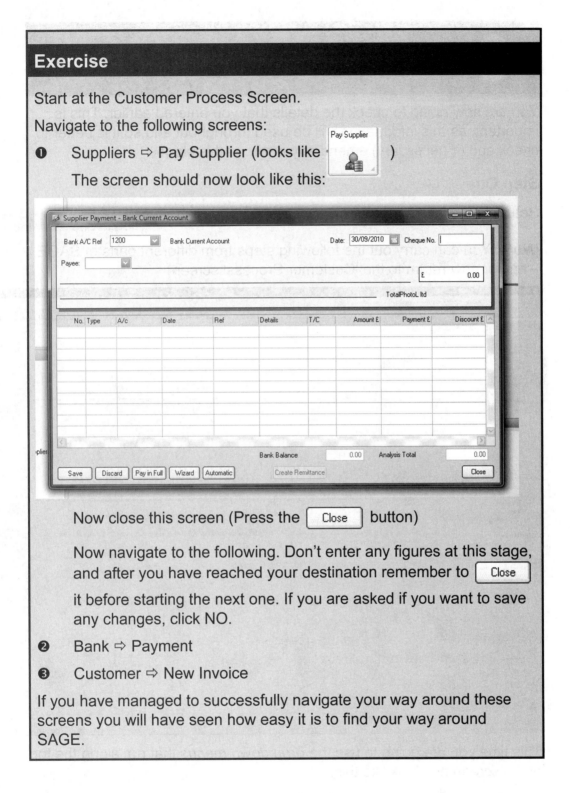)

The screen should now look like this:

Now close this screen (Press the [Close] button)

Now navigate to the following. Don't enter any figures at this stage, and after you have reached your destination remember to [Close] it before starting the next one. If you are asked if you want to save any changes, click NO.

❷ Bank ⇨ Payment

❸ Customer ⇨ New Invoice

If you have managed to successfully navigate your way around these screens you will have seen how easy it is to find your way around SAGE.

3 Checking your company details

You are now going to check the details that you entered earlier. This is important, as this information will be used throughout and so it is better to check and (if necessary) amend any errors at this stage.

Step One

Return to the 'Customer Process' screen by pressing

(*Note:* You can carry out the following steps from different parts of SAGE – but for now return to the 'Customer Process' screen)

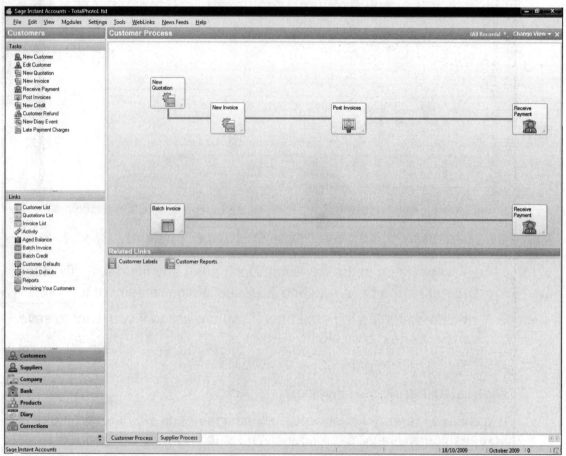

This time you are going to use the *drop down menus* that run along the top of the screen and look like this.

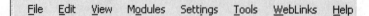

Click on **Settings,** and then from the menu select **Company Preferences.**

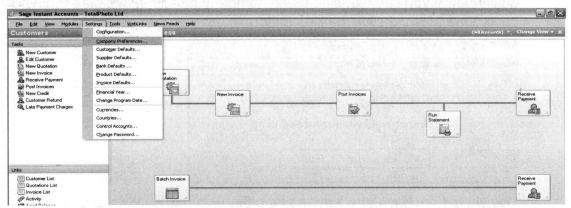

You will now see the company details that you input earlier. You should now thoroughly check these to make sure that they are correct.

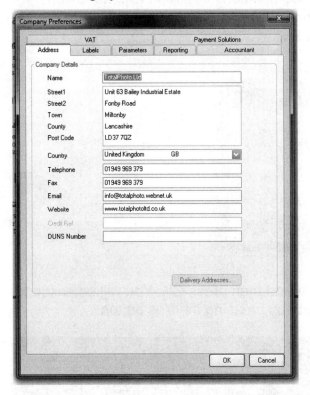

You can now also check the information you entered about the financial year is also correct.

Again using the *menus* at the top of the window, select **Settings** and then **Financial Year.**

You will now be warned that all other sections of SAGE must be closed down before you can examine these company details. Make sure that you have done this and click the Yes button.

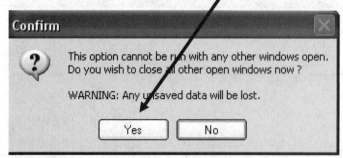

You should not have any data in any other sections at this point, and so you need not worry about losing it. ☺

REMEMBER – when we set up the company details in Chapter 3 you entered the financial year as running from October 2009. This should now be showing on the screen, as below.

Make sure this is the correct date and then press OK. You will be asked to double-check this – again, confirm by pressing the Yes button.

4 Dates

Your computer has an internal clock, which SAGE uses to set the default date and time every time you open the package. This is particularly important because the date at which SAGE records each transaction can have a significant effect on the accuracy of reports, calculation of VAT and so on.

However (and especially when you are practising) it can be a good idea to override this and to enter your own date in line with the case study materials you are working on. If you do this at the start, you will not need to keep re-entering the date when you are entering transactions.

To change the default date

Imagine that you are working on a practise exercise, and you are told that today's date is 30th April 2009. However, the *real date* is 4th December 2010.

The default date in SAGE for entering transactions will show as 4th December – and you would have to override this each and every time you made an entry. This is repetitive and increases the likelihood of making a mistake – entering "05" instead of "04", for example.

Fortunately SAGE allows you to change the default date. Simply select the SETTINGS menu, and then CHANGE PROGRAM DATE.

Now you can easily change the date to the date required by the assessment material – in this case 30th April 2009. Now, every time you enter a transaction in SAGE the date will default to 30th April. This will have no effect on your computer's internal clock, and the next time you use the program the default date will revert to the real date once more until you change it.

TASK

In the TotalPhoto Ltd Case Study, you are told that today's date is 30th September 2010. You should now change the default date on your computer to 30th September 2010. Remember that if you subsequently shut SAGE down, when you return to it you will need to change the default date again.

5 Checking your data

If you work steadily and carefully, you should not encounter many problems with your data entry. However, no matter how carefully you work, you will undoubtedly have to make corrections at some time – either because of human error in inputting data, or simply because new information comes to light.

One important feature of SAGE is the ability to check your data. This will help to identify any issues with data corruption (which can occur after a power cut, for example), missing data and date errors.

You can access the DataCheck facility by clicking on FILE in the main menu bar, then MAINTENANCE, and then CHECK DATA.

SAGE will check the validity of your data and advise you of any possible discrepancies.

You should note that the DataCheck facility will <u>not</u> identify data entry errors (e.g. entering the wring amount or posting to the wrong nominal code). The accuracy of data entry is your responsibility, and you should therefore aim to minimise the number of errors you make by being careful to check your work at all stages.

6 Making corrections

Many people are understandably a little nervous when using a computer system for the first time. They worry that they may break the system, or make mistakes that cannot be corrected.

Don't worry: SAGE offers a number of easy ways to amend or wipe errors.

These are covered in more detail later, but for now let us look at one of the more common mistakes that you may make – the simple (but frustrating!) entry of an incorrect figure.

KAPLAN PUBLISHING

Example

Imagine you are entering a purchase of some stationery for £10.00. In error, you enter £100.00, and post the transaction into the system before you notice your mistake. What should you do?

To start with, don't panic!

One of the great advantages of a computerised system is that most errors are easy to correct. In SAGE, many amendments are carried out using the MAINTENANCE – CORRECTIONS function.

Click on FILE in the main menu bar, then on MAINTENANCE, and finally CORRECTIONS.

You will now see a list of all the transactions you have entered in chronological order which can be amended

You now have two choices; you can either AMEND a previously-entered transaction, or DELETE it completely.

In the example above, you would simply want to amend the transaction. You could choose to amend the purchaser or supplier code, the product description, or the reference and date. In order to change other aspects of the transaction, such as the nominal code, the amounts or the VAT rate, you should click on the EDIT button.

It is relatively straightforward to correct most errors in this way; however, some errors require a different approach. These are covered in more detail later.

 7 Backing up your work

It is important that you save your data regularly, to guard against accidental losses which can prove very costly and time-consuming to recover or re-input.

Backing up your data should become part of your daily routine.

From the File menu at the top of the screen select 'Backup'.

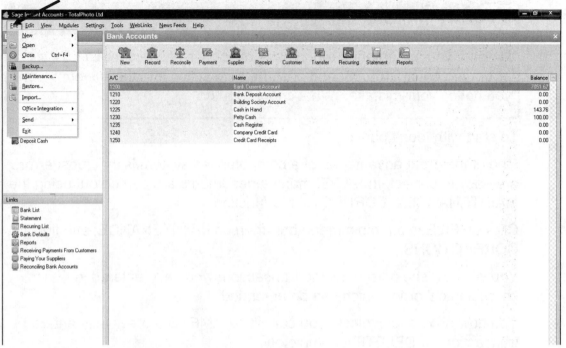

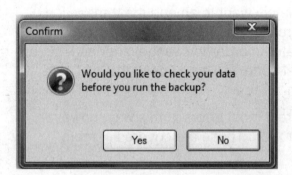

SAGE now asks if you would like to check your data before you run the backup – you should select [Yes]

Hopefully there are no problems with your data files and so you will now be able to backup your data.

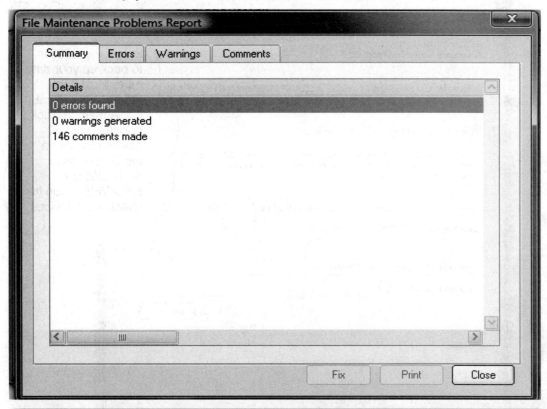

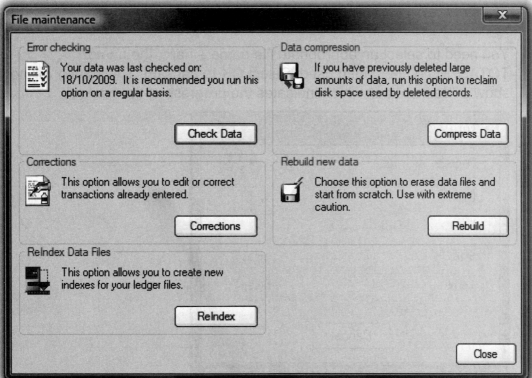

From this screen press the [Close] button to begin backup.

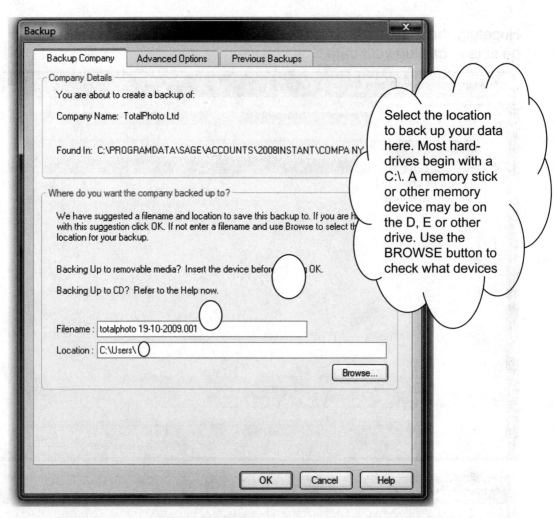

You need to select an appropriate file name – here, the name TOTALPHOTO has been used. Select **OK** to back up. The screen will now show a "Backup" box which indicates the progress of the backup.

When this process has finished SAGE will tell you that backup has been successfully completed and you can click **OK**.

You should note as well that SAGE invites you to backup your data each time you close the program down – the process is identical to that described above.

Setting up your suppliers' details 5

Introduction

Most business organisations will, over time, deal with a wide range of suppliers. A café may have different suppliers for their meat, cheese, vegetables, wine etc. A hairdresser will buy different products from different suppliers. Sometimes supplies will be obtained from a *wholesaler* or a *cash and carry*; other supplies may be sourced directly from the *manufacturers.*

The organisation will need to keep very accurate and timely records of all transactions with their suppliers. These transactions will typically include:

(1) Purchases and returns

(2) Discounts received from the supplier

(3) Payments made to the supplier in settlement of outstanding bills

In addition, it would be very convenient to have all the contact details of every supplier easily to hand.

Fortunately SAGE provides a very comprehensive Supplier management system which covers all these requirements (and more). You will see how this works shortly, but firstly you will need to enter your suppliers' details.

KNOWLEDGE	CONTENTS
1.2 Set up and create new accounting data records accurately to meet requirements	1 Supplier data
	2 Entering supplier details
1.3 Locate and display accounting data records to meet requirements	3 Entering detailed invoices or nil balances
	4 Printing supplier data reports

1 Supplier data

TotalPhoto Ltd has six suppliers, whose details are given below:

Mackay Films Ltd   A/c Ref : MF001
33 West Parade
Miltonby
Lancashire
LN87 7HD

Tel 01828 827493

Contact: Carl Richardson

Outstanding Balance at 30th September 2010: **£345.36**

Credit Terms: **30 days, 2% 7 days**   Credit Limit **£2,500**

K2 Films Ltd   A/c Ref : KF001
Tokyo House
72-84 Great Milne Street
London
WC4 6DD

Tel 0207 867 6599

Contact: Kim Nakajima

Outstanding Balance at 30th September 2010: **£1,726.55**

Credit Terms: **30 days, 2% 7 days**   Credit Limit **£5,000**

The Stationery Cupboard   A/c Ref : SC003
21 Potter Way
Hull
Humberside
HU87 6YY

Tel 01482 417378

Contact: Alan Pensill

Outstanding Balance at 30th September 2010: **£375.00**

Credit Terms: **14 days, no settlement discount**   Credit Limit **£1,000**

KAPLAN PUBLISHING

Mills Paper Products A/c Ref : MP002
405 Ream Road
Bradford
West Yorkshire
YO30 P08

Tel 01726 378918

Contact: Mr Shaun Squire

Outstanding Balance at 30th September 2010: **£4,920.30**

Credit Terms: **21 days, 1% 7 days** **Credit Limit £8,000**

Octopus Inks Ltd A/c Ref : OI001
Unit 12
Longley Industrial Park
Gateshead
Tyne and Wear
GH77 5TG

Tel 0191 252 4132

Contact: Sheila Cribbley

Outstanding Balance at 30th September 2010: **£550.20**

Credit Terms: **30 days, 2.5% 10 days** **Credit Limit £2,500**

Arthur's Photographic Equipment Ltd A/c Ref : AP004
77 Overton Lane
Birmingham
BM97 8YK

Tel 0121 299 0192

Contact: Jennie Reeves

Outstanding Balance at 30th September 2010: **£11,275.00**

Credit Terms: **30 days, 1% 7 days** **Credit Limit £20,000**

2 Entering supplier details

From the Supplier Process window (below) press the **New Supplier** task.

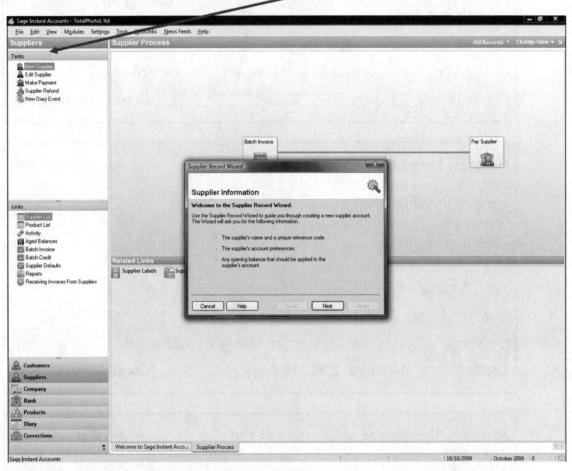

This will bring up the **Supplier Record Wizard**, which will help you to easily enter your suppliers' details.

To continue with this you will need to refer to the list of suppliers for TotalPhoto Ltd on the previous pages.

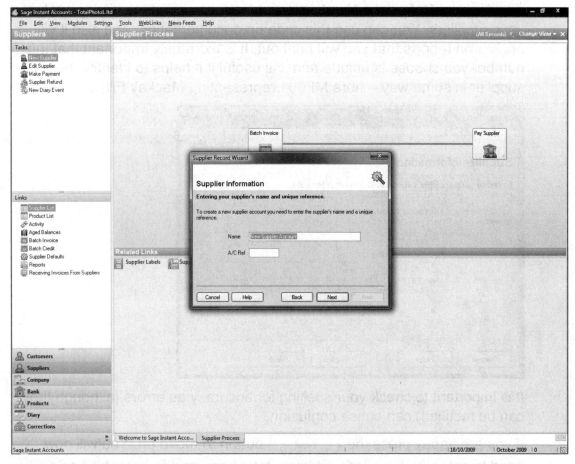

The first supplier to enter from page 42 is:

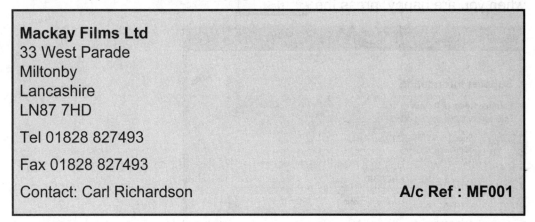

Mackay Films Ltd
33 West Parade
Miltonby
Lancashire
LN87 7HD

Tel 01828 827493

Fax 01828 827493

Contact: Carl Richardson   **A/c Ref : MF001**

To complete the first screen of the **New Supplier Wizard** you will need to enter the supplier's name (Mackay Films Ltd) and their unique Account Reference Number (A/C Ref – MF001).

The Account Reference Number is a shorthand way of identifying each of your suppliers. You can use this code on documentation, and also it will appear on reports that you will print out. It is extremely important that the number you choose is unique and it is useful if it helps to identify the supplier in some way – here MF001 representing **M**ackay **F**ilms.

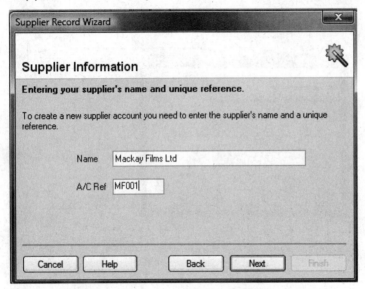

It is important to check your spelling for accuracy as errors (although they can be rectified) can cause confusion.

If you are happy press the [Next] button to move on. You will now need to enter the supplier's address, telephone and fax details. Again, when you are happy, press the [Next]

Now you can enter the firm's contact details. In this case we have not got an e-mail or website address, or the VAT number. Don't worry, though, as these can easily be entered at a later date. You can enter Carl Richardson's name at this point, though, before pressing the Next button.

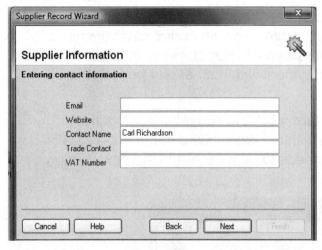

The next screen asks you to enter details of your credit terms with this supplier, the nominal code against which purchases from this supplier will be recorded, and also the most common VAT rating for the goods that you buy from them.

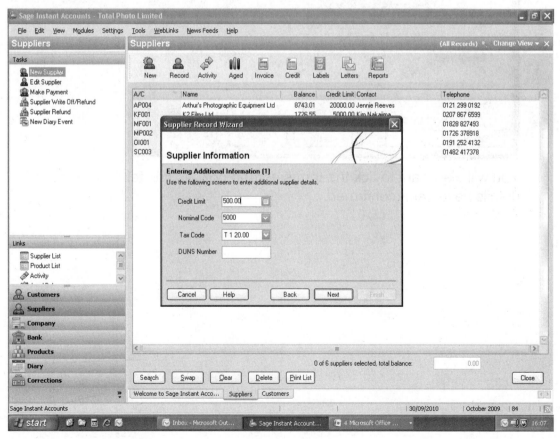

Here we can enter the credit limit of £2500. The nominal code is 5000 (you will learn more about nominal codes later) and the VAT code is T1, meaning that the majority of purchases from this supplier will have VAT added at 17.5%.

If you are happy with this press the | Next | button.

Now you can enter details of any credit terms that the supplier offers. Most suppliers will insist on payment within a certain period of time – typically seven to twenty eight days **(the payment days).** However, some suppliers may also offer a discount for payment within an earlier period **(the settlement days)**.

Mackay Films Ltd offer credit terms of **"2% 7days"** meaning that if TotalPhoto Ltd settle invoices within 7 days they can deduct a 2% discount from the amount owing. This needs to be reflected in the next window as shown below.

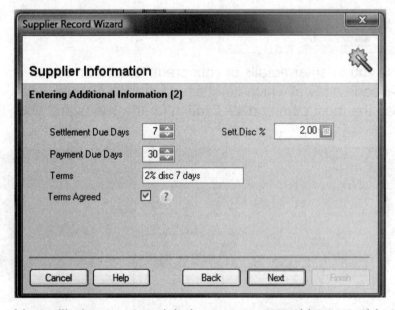

You will also want to tick the terms agreed box, as this tells Sage that the details have been confirmed.

The next screens ask you to enter the details of your supplier's bank. This is essential if you will be paying the supplier using methods such as BACS. It is not necessary if you will always be paying by cheque – but we have the information available and so can enter it.

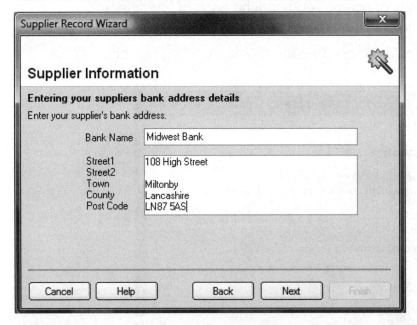

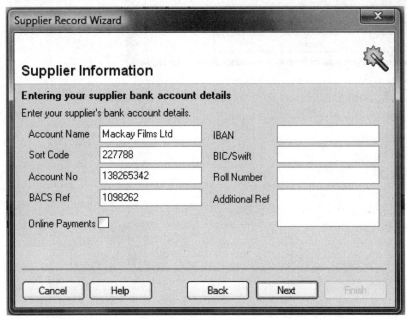

SAGE now asks if this supplier has an outstanding balance – in other words, if at the time of entering their details you already owe them money. In this example, TotalPhoto Ltd currently owes Mackay Films Ltd £345.36. This figure can be entered either as one figure, or alternatively could be entered as a series of figures representing each of the different outstanding invoices at the time of entry.

For now, you should choose to enter the outstanding balance as one figure.

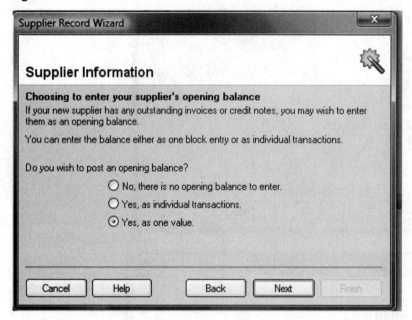

Remember today's date is 30th September 2010. This is therefore the date that we will be entering our opening balances. On the following screen either type the date (30/09/2010) or use SAGE's calendar facility to enter it, as shown below.

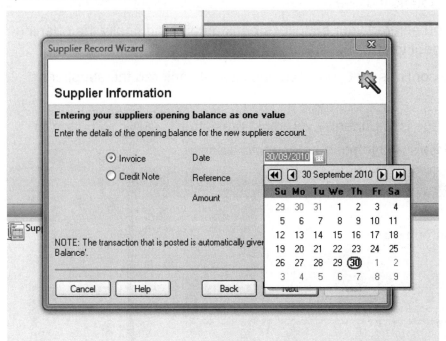

You can now also enter the opening balance for Mackay Films Ltd. Check your entries then press the Next button.

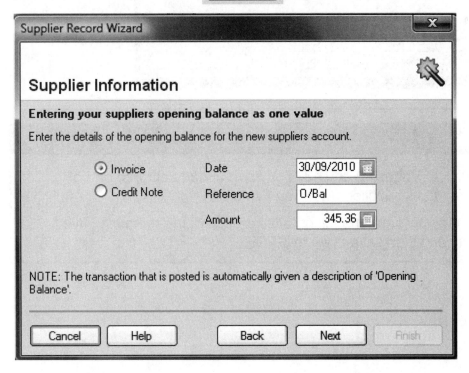

Well done! You have now entered your first supplier details. To recap, you began by entering their company details, such as their address, phone and fax numbers and contact details. Then you entered the credit terms that this supplier makes available to us, including normal payment terms and any discounts that are available for early settlement.

After that you entered your supplier's bank details and finally the opening balance of debt to that supplier.

SAGE now confirms that you have successfully entered the supplier's details.

The next stage is important – you <u>must</u> press the [Finish] button to save the details and to post the opening balance.

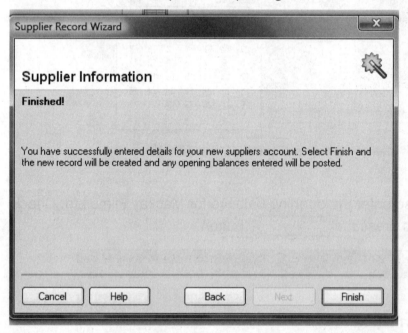

Exercise

Refer back to Pages 42 and 43. You have already entered one of TotalPhoto Ltd's suppliers (Mackay Films Ltd).

You should now enter the full details for each of the remaining five suppliers, and then save them to SAGE.

3 Entering detailed invoices or nil balances

When you entered the opening balances for TotalPhoto's suppliers, you simply entered them as one amount. In reality, of course, these opening balances are likely to be made up of a number of different outstanding invoices, along perhaps with one or more credit notes. If this is the case, it would be useful to record each outstanding invoice separately, so that it can be referred to when payment is eventually received. In order to do this, you would simply click the button labelled "Yes, as individual transactions".

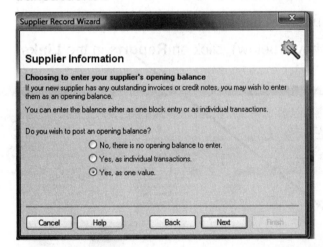

You will now be able to enter each outstanding invoice or credit note individually.

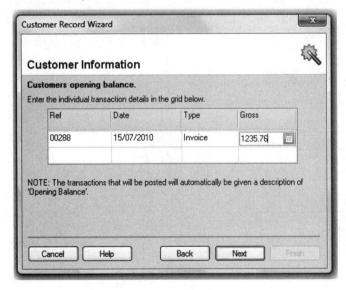

Entering Zero Balances

Sometimes an existing supplier will have no outstanding invoices at the date they are entered into the system. In this situation, simply click on the "No, there is no opening balance to enter" button.

4 Printing supplier data reports

You have entered the details of the six suppliers, so let's now check that they are correct by running off a report from SAGE.

The first report to print is the Supplier List.

From the **Suppliers** window (shown below), click on **Reports** in the **Links** area.

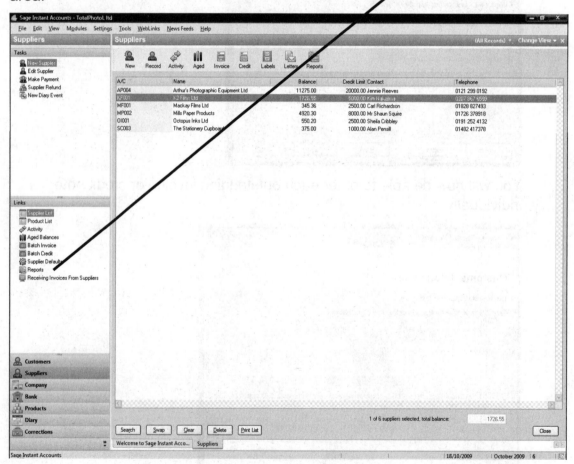

This will produce a new window with a list of supplier-related reports that you could want to print and use. You will practice accessing some more of these later on, but for now the one that you want is the report entitled *Supplier Address List*. This is contained within the folder called *Supplier Details Reports* – to access the contents of this (or any) folder simply click on the + sign to the side of the folder name to expand it to show its contents.

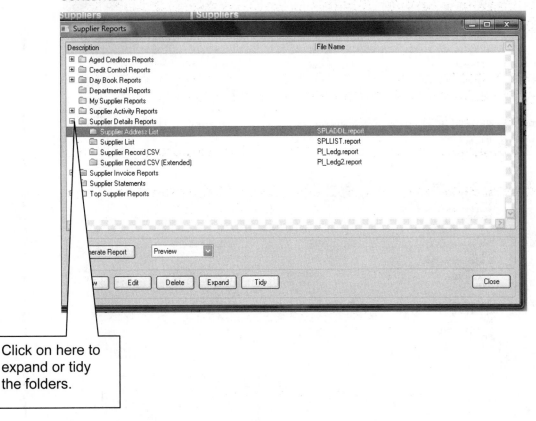

Click on here to expand or tidy the folders.

Double click on *Supplier Address List* to produce the report.

On the next screen you can identify the criteria by which you wish to select the contents of your report. As you wish to see a list of all the suppliers that you have entered keep the boxes as shown below, then press OK.

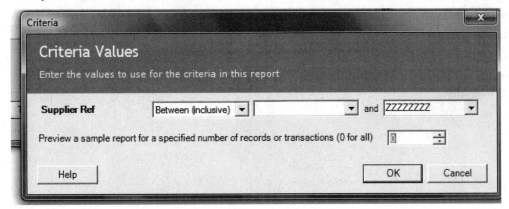

Your report should now show on screen, similar to the one below.

Date:	18/10/2009		**TotalPhoto Ltd**		Page:	1
Time:	11:55:33		**Supplier Address List**			

Supplier From:
Supplier To: ZZZZZZZZ

A/C	Name	Contact	Telephone	Fax
AF004	Arthur's Photographic Equipment Ltd 77 Overton Lane Birmingham BM97 8YK	Jennie Reeves	0121 299 0192	
KF001	K2 Films Ltd Tokyo House 72-84 Great Milne Street London WC4 6DD	Kim Nakajima	0207 867 6599	
MF001	Mackay Films Ltd 33 West Parade Miltonby Lancashire LN87 7HD	Carl Richardson	01828 827493	
MP002	Mills Paper Products 405 Ream Road Bradford West Yorkshire YO30 P08	Mr Shaun Squire	01726 378918	
OI001	Octopus Inks Ltd Unit 12 Longley Industrial Park Gateshead Tyne and Wear GH77 5TG	Sheila Cribbley	0191 252 4132	
SC003	The Stationery Cupboard 21 Potter Way Hull Humberside HU87 6YY	Alan Persill	01482 417378	

There are many other supplier reports available in this section – you should now feel confident enough to access these and to print them out. The exact list of reports that you will use will depend on your particular requirements, and you will see some of the more common ones later in this manual.

Setting up your customers' details

Introduction

Now that you have successfully entered your suppliers' details you can now move on to enter relevant information about your customers as well.

The process of entering your customers' details is very similar to that of entering supplier information, so you should feel confident doing this now.

It is of course vitally important that you keep accurate records for each of your customers. This information is likely to include:

(1)   Sales made on credit to customers, and sales returns

(2)   Credit terms for your customers, including any discount they may receive

(3)   Contact details for easy invoicing

(4)   Payments received from customers

Consistent, accurate recording of information is a vital aspect of any credit management system, ensuring that your organisation gets paid as quickly as possible for its sales. This can be the difference between failure and survival for most businesses.

KNOWLEDGE
1.2   Set up and create new accounting data records accurately to meet requirements
1.3   Locate and display accounting data records to meet requirements

CONTENTS
1   Customer data
2   Printing customer data reports

1 Customer data

TotalPhoto Ltd has six customers with outstanding balances as at 30th September 2010. Their details are given below:

Mr W Haslam
22 Brown Street
Miltonby
Lancashire
LN87 6FD

A/c Ref : HAS004

Amount outstanding at 30th September 2010: £309.85

Credit terms: Payment in 14 days   Credit limit: £500

Mrs H Poppy
120 Forrest Way
Miltonby
Lancashire
LN87 9YR

A/c Ref : POP002

Amount outstanding at 30th September 2010: £220.00

Credit terms: Payment in 14 days   Credit limit: £500

Miss S Pargenter
11 Alexandra Park
Miltonby
Lancashire
LN87 2WD

A/c Ref: PAR006

Amount outstanding at 30th September 2010: £650.00

Credit terms: Payment in 14 days   Credit limit: £1000

Mrs T Pashby
30A Andrews Street
Killington
Lancashire
LN85 6TT

A/c Ref: PAS002

Amount outstanding at 30th September 2010:   £89.50

Credit terms: Payment in 14 days   Credit limit: £500

Campbell & Dunn Ltd
12 The Beeches
Miltonby
Lancashire
LN87 9PP

A/c Ref: CAM004

Amount outstanding at 30th September 2010:   £2056.85

Credit terms: 14 days, 1% in 7 days   Credit limit: £2500

Lullabies Nursery
104 Victoria Road
Miltonby
Lancashire
LN87 5PS

A/c Ref: LUL002

Amount outstanding at 30th September 2010:   £726.90

Credit terms: Payment in 14 days   Credit limit: £1500

You will now enter these six customer details into SAGE.

Step One

Go to the Customer Process screen, as below.

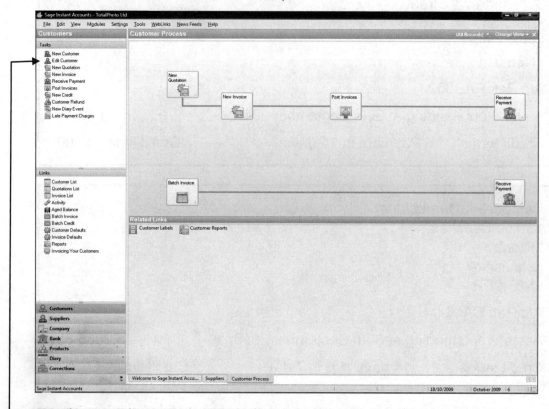

From the Task Bar, click on New Customer. At the next screen click NEXT, and you should now be able to enter your first customer's details, as below.

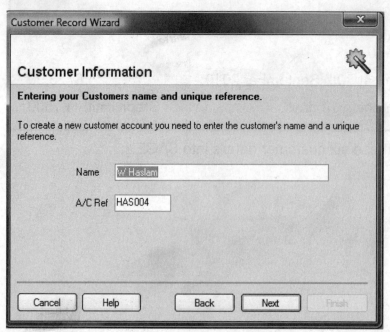

When you have done this click the NEXT button again, and enter the address details, as below.

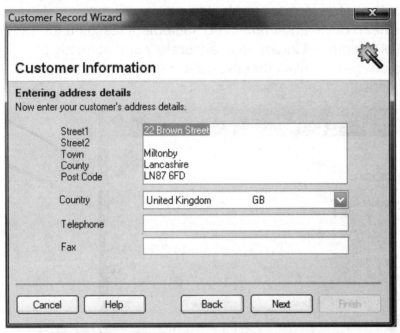

As with the supplier entry process, the next screen will ask you for further contact details, such as email and website addresses. You do not need to enter any information here at this point, so press the NEXT button.

Now you can enter the credit limit for this customer (this represents the maximum value of goods or services we are prepared to sell to them on credit) Here, for Mr Haslam, it is £500.

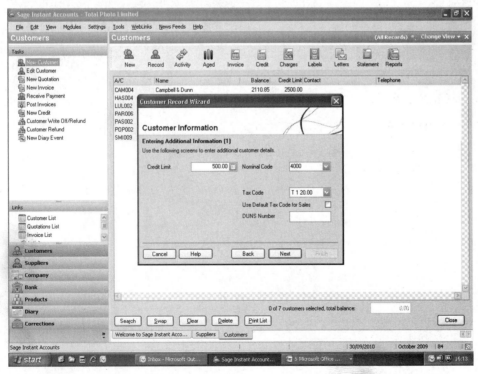

Leave the nominal code as 4000, and the tax code as T1 (17.50), as in the screen above. You will learn more about these shortly.

Now you can enter the credit terms. For Mr Haslam we will require payment within fourteen days, and there is no settlement discount for early payment. Be careful to enter all information accurately and correctly at every stage of this process – check that the details you have entered match the source data.

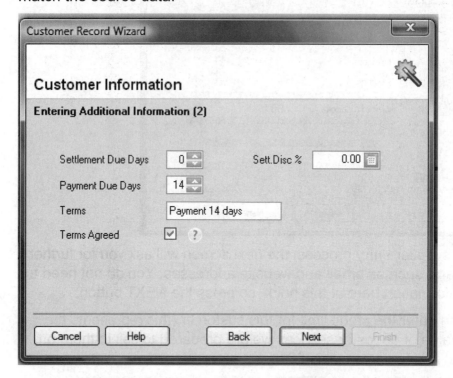

SAGE will now ask if there are any opening balances, and as with the supplier entry screen you can enter these in one of three ways. Again, you should choose to enter them as a single value.

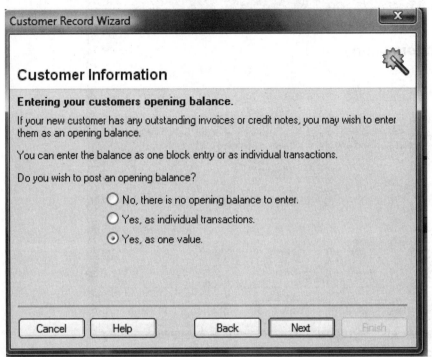

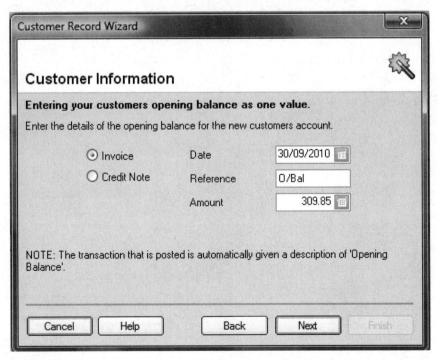

Enter the opening balance for Mr Haslam (£309.85) as above.

SAGE now asks you to confirm the details you have entered and to save them. Again, this is an important stage of the process.

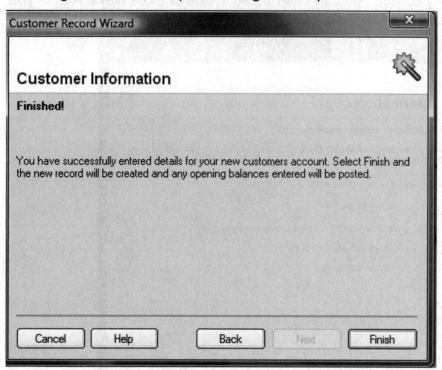

Click on the FINISH button to complete the process.

Activity

Refer back to Pages 58 and 59. You have already entered one of TotalPhoto Ltd's customers (Mr W Haslam).

You should now enter the full details for each of the remaining five customers, and then save them to SAGE. When you have done this your screen should look like this:

2 Printing customer data reports

You have entered the details of the six customers, so let's now check that they are correct by running off a report from SAGE.

The first report to print is the Customer List.

From the **Customers** window (shown below), click on **Reports** in the **Links** area.

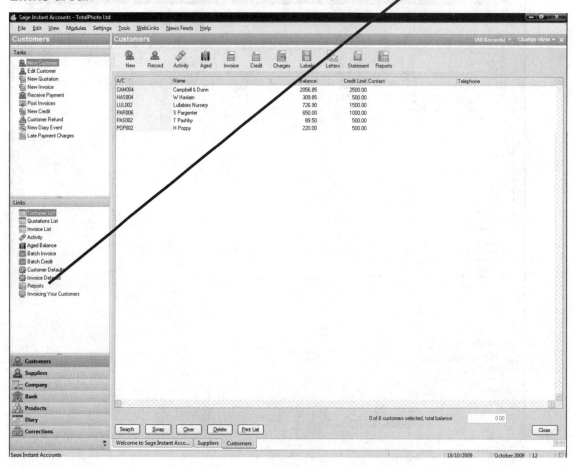

This will produce a new window with a list of customer-related reports that you could want to print and use. You will practice accessing some more of these later on, but for now the one that you want is the report entitled *Customer Address List*. This is contained within the folder called *Customer Details Reports* – to access the contents of this (or any) folder simply click on the + sign to the side of the folder name to expand it to show its contents.

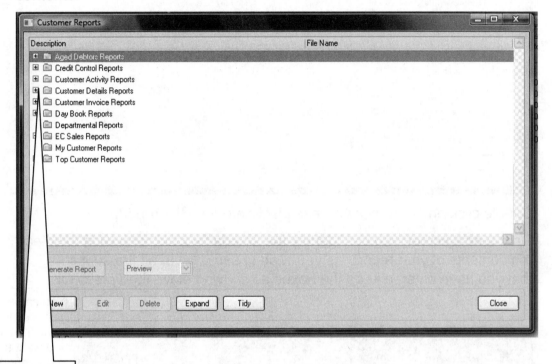

Click on here to expand or tidy the folders.

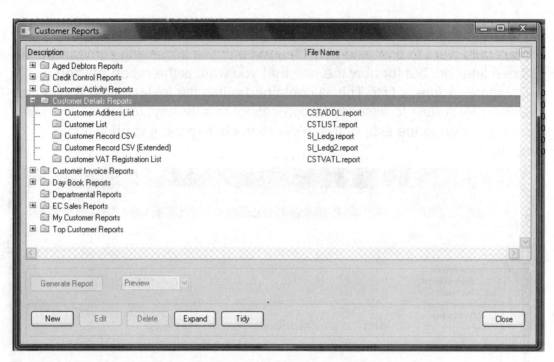

Double click on *Customer Address List* to produce the report.

On the next screen you can identify the criteria by which you wish to select the contents of your report. As you wish to see a list of all the suppliers that you have entered keep the boxes as shown below, then press OK.

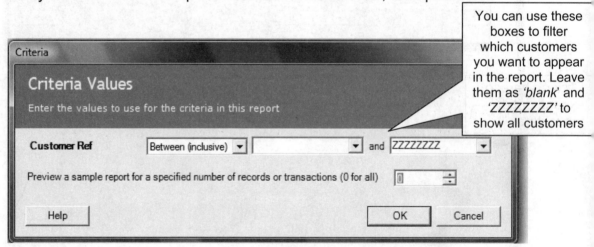

You can use these boxes to filter which customers you want to appear in the report. Leave them as *'blank'* and 'ZZZZZZZZ' to show all customers

Your report should now show on screen, similar to the one below.

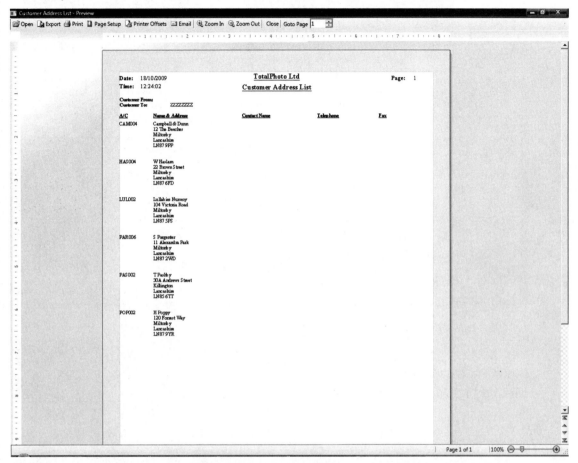

There are many other supplier reports available in this section – you should now feel confident enough to access these and to print them out. The exact list of reports that you will use will depend on your particular requirements, and you will see some of the more common ones later in this manual.

The nominal ledger

7

KNOWLEDGE

1.2 Set up and create new accounting data records accurately to meet requirements

1.3 Locate and display accounting data records to meet requirements

CONTENTS

1 Introduction

The nominal ledger is probably the most important element of the SAGE (or indeed any) accounting system. The key aspect to this is the list of nominal codes. This is simply a series of different accounts into which money is debited (paid in) or credited (taken out) each time a transaction is recorded.

Each of these accounts is given a unique four digit code number. To view the list of Nominal Codes go to the COMPANY screen, and then NOMINAL LEDGER.

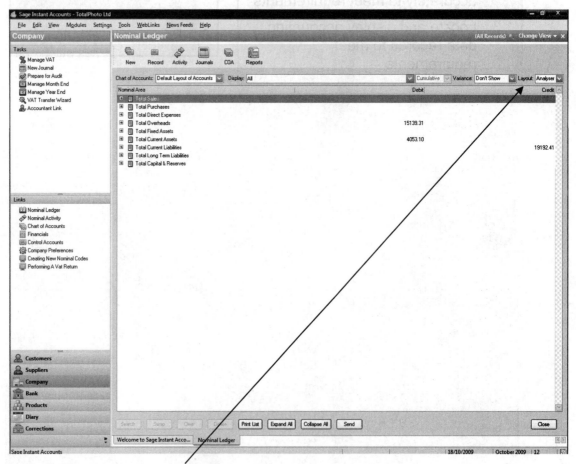

Select 'List' from the layout menu.

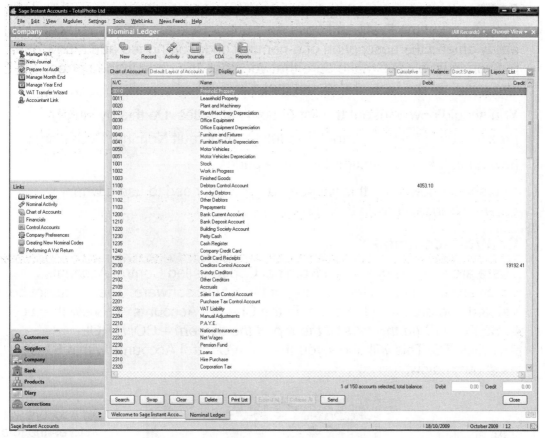

This now shows you a list of all of the nominal codes (N/Cs) for the business.

The four-digit code is important, as the list is actually broken down into groups:

0000-0999	Fixed Assets and Depreciation (e.g. Buildings, Equipment)
1000-1999	Current Assets (e.g. Stock, Debtors, Bank)
2000-2999	Liabilities (e.g. Loans, Creditors)
3000-3999	Capital and Reserves
4000-4999	Sales
5000-5999	Purchases
6000-6999	Direct Expenses (e.g. Direct Labour)
7000-7999	Miscellaneous Overheads (e.g. Phone, Rent, Postage)
8000-8999	Bad debts and Depreciation
9000-9999	Suspense and Mispostings

SAGE uses these 'groupings' of codes to ensure that items appear in the correct part of the Profit and Loss Account or Balance Sheet. You can easily amend the description of a nominal code, or indeed add a new one, but you must always make sure that you keep the code in the correct 'grouping' for the type of account that it is.

You should now print out the list of nominal codes. Do this by simply pressing the Print List button. The full list of default Nominal Codes should now print, taking approximately three pages.

You should now keep this list safe, as you will need to use it when entering transactions in the future.

Control Accounts

There are some very special Nominal Codes called Control Accounts, which are essential to the running of the SAGE software. These cannot be deleted and are always present in the Chart of Accounts. To view them go to SETTINGS *(in the tabs at the top of the screen)* – CONTROL ACCOUNTS. This will show you the main Control Accounts within SAGE, as shown below.

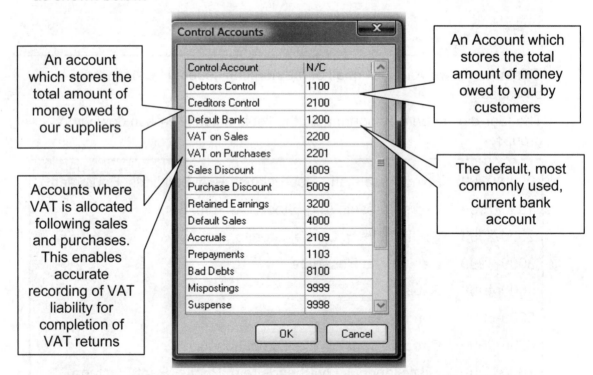

Most of these accounts are used automatically by SAGE. This means that you do not need to specify them individually when entering transactions – SAGE will work out which control account is required and apply it automatically. Other Nominal Codes (from the list you printed out) will need to be entered.

2 Entering a nominal code

The default Chart of Accounts contains the most common codes set up for a general business. However, you will almost certainly want to add to, or amend, these Nominal Codes to suit your business in particular.

For example, TotalPhoto Ltd will want to be more specific when recording its sales and purchases. Have a look at your listing of Nominal Codes. Find the 5000-5999 Range (remember, these are set aside for Purchases).

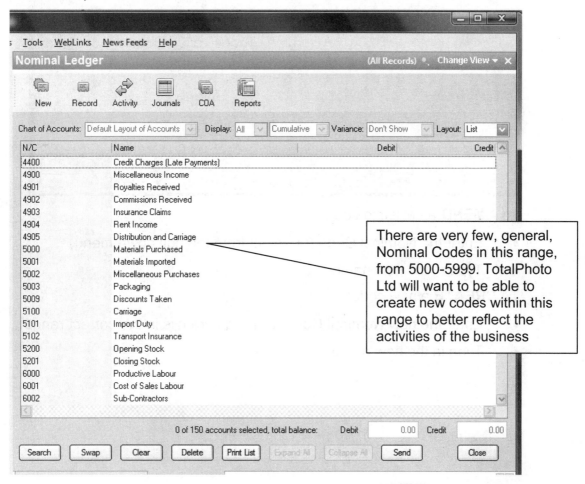

Now, from within the NOMINAL module click on the Record button.

You should now have a blank record screen, as below.

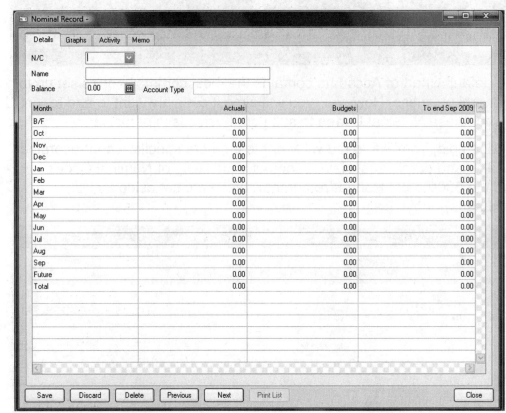

To **AMEND** an existing code:

- Enter the Nominal Code (or select from the pull down menu)
- Type in the new name

To **CREATE** a new code:

- Enter the new Nominal Code (making sure it is in the correct range)
- Type in the new name

Exercise

To practice amending and creating Nominal Codes, enter each of the following N/Cs and names. Do them one by one, and then save each one.

SALES		PURCHASES	
Nominal Code	*Name*	*Nominal Code*	*Name*
4000	Individuals and Family	5000	Purchases - Film
4001	Weddings	5001	Purchases - Paper
4002	Corporate	5002	Purchases - Cartridges & toner
4003	Nurseries & Schools	5003	Purchases - Stationery
4004	Other Sales	5004	Purchases - Other consumables

Once you have entered these, close down the window and generate the Nominal List report for the range 4000-5999. This should now look like this:

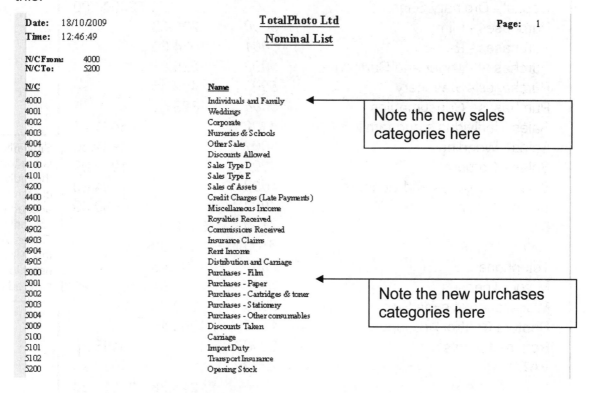

Date:	18/10/2009		
Time:	12:46:49		

TotalPhoto Ltd
Nominal List
Page: 1

N/C From: 4000
N/C To: 5200

N/C	Name
4000	Individuals and Family
4001	Weddings
4002	Corporate
4003	Nurseries & Schools
4004	Other Sales
4009	Discounts Allowed
4100	Sales Type D
4101	Sales Type E
4200	Sales of Assets
4400	Credit Charges (Late Payments)
4900	Miscellaneous Income
4901	Royalties Received
4902	Commissions Received
4903	Insurance Claims
4904	Rent Income
4905	Distribution and Carriage
5000	Purchases - Film
5001	Purchases - Paper
5002	Purchases - Cartridges & toner
5003	Purchases - Stationery
5004	Purchases - Other consumables
5009	Discounts Taken
5100	Carriage
5101	Import Duty
5102	Transport Insurance
5200	Opening Stock

Note the new sales categories here

Note the new purchases categories here

Well done! Now you can amend or create new nominal codes. The next step is to post opening balances to each relevant nominal code within SAGE for your business. This means that you will be entering the financial balance on each account for TotalPhoto Ltd, as at the first date you begin using the SAGE system to record financial transactions for the company. Remember for TotalPhoto Ltd this was 30th September 2010. The list of opening balances is shown below:

TotalPhoto Ltd

Opening Balances

	Nominal code	Debit	Credit
Motor vehicles (at cost)	0050	21800.00	
Depreciation (Motor Vehicles)	0051		5450.00
Office Equipment	0030	4849.00	
Depreciation (Office Equipment)	0031		921.00
Photographic Equipment	0022	22718.00	
Depreciation (Photo Eqpmt)	0023		4316.00
Stock (as at 1st October 2009)	1001	7403.00	
Petty Cash	1230	250.00	
Bank	1200	10293.00	
Creditors Control Account	2100		19192.41
Capital - Ordinary Shares	3000		20000.00
Purchases - Film	5000	205.63	
Purchases - Paper	5001	1034.35	
Purchases - Toner and Cartridges	5002	1225.87	
Purchases - Stationery	5003	409.35	
Purchases - Consumables	5004	823.52	
Sales - Individuals and families	4000		5401.21
Sales - Weddings	4001		3984.50
Sales - Corporate	4002		1932.09
Sales - Nurseries and Schools	4003		11304.20
Sales - Other	4004		1590.30
Rent	7100	3800.00	
Rates	7103	480.00	
Telephone	7502	603.43	
Motor expenses	7304	1035.64	
Miscellaneous expenses	6900	229.39	
Debtors Control Account	1100	4053.10	
Retained profits	3200		5498.28
VAT	2202		1623.29
		81213.28	81213.28

Note: this is the total of the suppliers' balances that you entered earlier. This has already been entered and so will not need to be entered again

Similarly this is the total of the individual customers' accounts that you entered earlier. Again, this will not need to be entered again

Entering a new balance

Entering opening balances in SAGE is very straightforward.

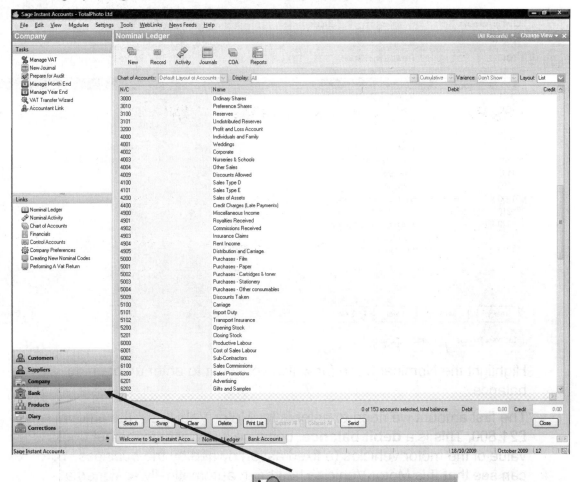

From the main screen click on the **Company** button.
This will bring up the Nominal Ledger screen, as shown below.

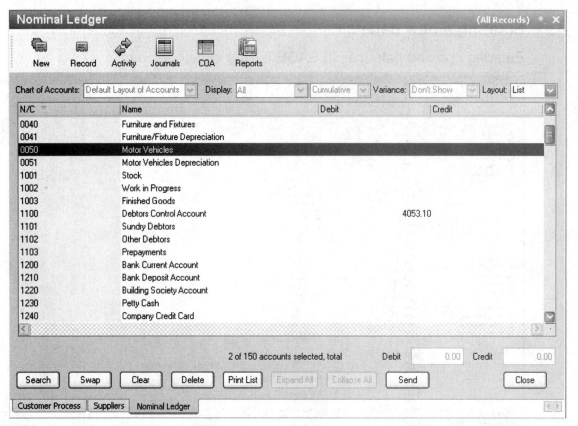

Highlight the Nominal Code for which you want to enter an opening balance.

The first amount we need to enter is for Motor Vehicles – the amount is £21,800. This is a **debit balance**, because it represents the net book value of the motor vehicles (a fixed asset) owned by the business. You can see that this Motor Vehicles has been automatically assigned a Nominal Code of **0050** by SAGE.

Double-click your mouse on this code.

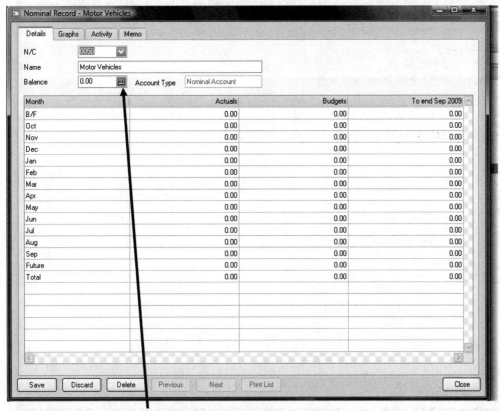

Now click on the 'Opening Balance' icon.

Keep the Ref as "O/Bal". Change the date box to 30th September 2010, and enter the opening balance amount of £21,800.00 in the Debit box. Leave the credit box at zero. Then click the Save button.

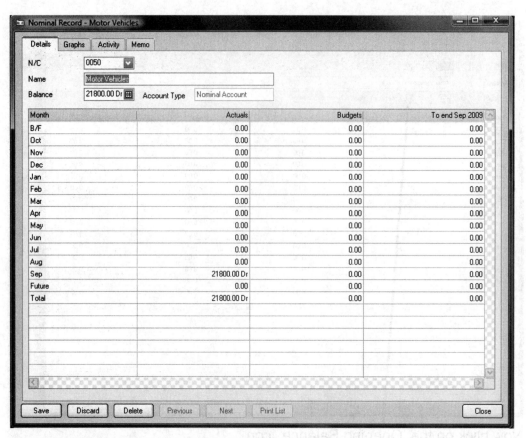

Notice how the detail record for Nominal Code 0050 (Motor Vehicles) has now changed, showing your entry in September. When you return to the Nominal Ledger page you should also see the new balance reflected there.

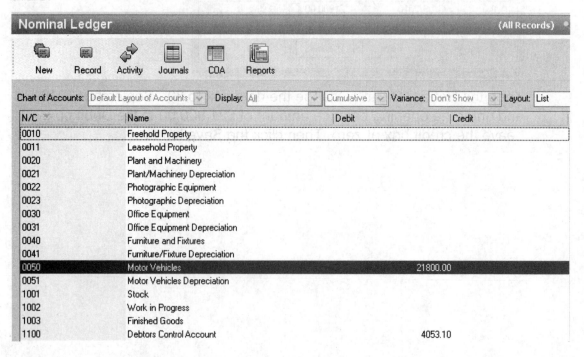

Exercise

You should now be able to enter the opening balances for each of the accounts.

Important

1   You will need to create new Nominal Codes for three items: Photographic Equipment, Depreciation of Photographic Equipment, and Miscellaneous Expenses.

2   You do not need to enter opening balances for two items, the Debtors Control Account and the Creditors Control Account. This is because these represent the total amount owed to us (debtors) and the total amount we owe (creditors), made up of all of the individual balances you entered earlier. These control account balances are therefore calculated automatically by SAGE and you do not enter them.

3   Be careful to enter each balance correctly as either a **debit** or a **credit** balance.

3 Printing a trial balance

You have now entered all the opening balances for TotalPhoto Ltd. You are now ready to begin entering transactions on a day to day basis. Before that though, you should print off a Trial Balance.

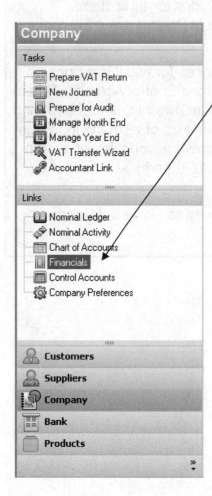

From the Company screen, select "Financials" in the links section.

This will create a new screen, from which you can quickly produce a series of the most useful reports in SAGE, including the Trial Balance, the Balance Sheet and the Profit and Loss Account. Double-click on 'Financials' to show this screen.

From the toolbar at the top of the Financials screen:

Select the 🔘 Trial icon.

You are now asked to select how you want to view the report.

For now, you will just preview the report (i.e. view it on screen). Highlight this and the press the [Run] button.

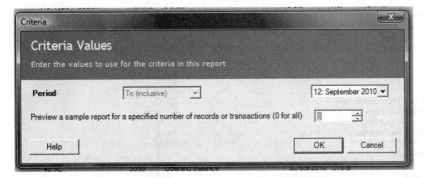

You want to view the trial balance as at September 2010, to see all of the opening balances you have entered. Make sure you amend the date box to show September 2010. Leave the next box as 0, and click [OK]

This should bring up a trial balance showing balances for the period up to September 2010. You may need to maximize the screen to see the whole report on screen – do this by clicking the *maximize* icon in the top right corner of the window ([□])

If you have entered everything correctly you should see that both columns (debit and credit) balance to £81,213.28.

You should now print out this trial balance and keep it safe.

Date:	02/07/2012	**Total Photo Limited**	Page:	1
Time:	12:23:02	**Period Trial Balance**		

To Period: Month 12, September 2010

N/C	Name	Debit	Credit
0022	Photographic Equipment	22,718.00	
0023	Depreciation (Photo Equipment)		4,316.00
0030	Office Equipment	4,849.00	
0031	Office Equipment Depreciation		921.00
0050	Motor Vehicles	21,800.00	
0051	Motor Vehicles Depreciation		5,450.00
1001	Stock	7,403.00	
1100	Debtors Control Account	4,053.10	
1200	Bank Current Account	10,293.00	
1230	Petty Cash	250.00	
2100	Creditors Control Account		19,192.41
2202	VAT Liability		1,623.29
3000	Capital		20,000.00
3200	Retained profits		5,498.28
4000	Sales - Individuals and Family		5,401.21
4001	Sales - Weddings		3,984.50
4002	Sales - Corporate		1,932.09
4003	Sales - Nurseries & Schools		11,304.20
4004	Other Sales		1,590.30
5000	Purchases - Film	205.63	
5001	Purchases - Paper	1,034.35	
5002	Purchases - Cartridges & toner	1,225.87	
5003	Purchases - Stationery	409.35	
5004	Purchases - Other consumables	823.52	
6900	Miscellaneous Expenses	229.39	
7100	Rent	3,800.00	
7103	General Rates	480.00	
7304	Miscellaneous Motor Expenses	1,035.64	
7502	Telephone	603.43	
	Totals:	81,213.28	81,213.28

This shows what your trial balance should look like after entering all of the opening balances.

If you have managed to follow this manual so far, and produce a trial balance to match the above – Well Done! You are now ready to move on.

Entering transactions

1   Introduction

Any business will carry out a wide range of transactions every day of the week. However, the majority of these will fall into one of the following categories:

Credit transactions

•   Purchases of stock on credit

•   Sales of goods or services on credit

Cash transactions

•   Purchases made by cash/cheque/card

•   Sales made for cash/cheque/card

•   Payments made to suppliers (for goods/services bought on credit)

•   Receipts from customers (for goods/services sold on credit)

•   Payments made to meet other expenses

•   Payment of salaries and wages to staff

•   Petty cash transactions

•   Transactions directly through the bank account (e.g. bank charges, interest, direct debits, standing order)

Each of these transactions will have an effect on two accounts within the SAGE system – this is the underlying principle of double-entry bookkeeping. However, SAGE simplifies this by carrying out much of the double entry automatically.

Consider firstly the first transactions – purchases and sales made on credit. This means that a legally binding contract is established between the two parties, and (usually) the goods or services are supplied but payment is not paid until some later date. The key document in this process is the **invoice** – as this is the document which demands payment and lays down the agreed terms of the transaction.

Hence entering a credit transaction (whether a purchase or a sale) is a two stage process in SAGE:

1   Enter the details of the invoice against the relevant supplier or customer. This will establish the presence and value of the legally binding debt.

2   At a later date, enter the details of the payment of the debt.

Note that this approach is applicable for both credit sales and credit purchases – you just have to be sure to enter the details in the correct part of SAGE.

Now consider the second transactions – each of these has a direct impact on one or other of the bank accounts within SAGE. Note that SAGE classes accounts such as cash in hand and petty cash as *'bank accounts'* – they are all current assets within the Balance Sheet.

2 Credit sales – batching customer invoices

TotalPhoto Ltd have had a number of credit customers on 30th September. Each of this has been issued with an invoice, but these invoices now need to be entered into SAGE.

The easiest way to do this is to *batch* invoices together so that they can be input at the same time.

To enter a batch of customer (sales) invoices go to the **CUSTOMERS**

module and then press the **BATCH INVOICE** button

You will now need to insert data into the next screen as follows:

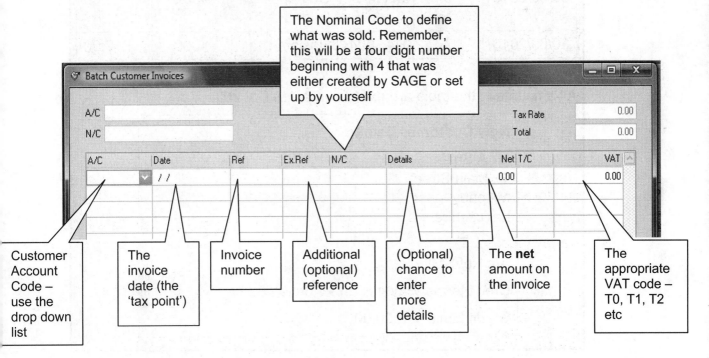

Once you have entered all invoices in the batch you should then review them to ensure you have entered them correctly, and then [Save] them. This will post the invoices to SAGE and update the system accordingly.

Exercise

Enter the following six invoices for TotalPhoto Ltd using the batch invoicing method. Note that you will also have to create new customer accounts in some cases.

Date	Invoice No	A/c No	Customer	Nominal Code	Amount
30/09/2010	1	POP002	Poppy	4000	£105.00
30/09/2010	2	HAS004	Haslam	4000	£24.50
30/09/2010	3	PAR006	Pargenter	4000	£12.00
30/09/2010	4	SMI009	Smith (see below)	4001	£600.00
30/09/2010	5	LUL002	Lullabies Nursery	4003	£100.00
30/09/2010	6	CAM004	Campbell & Dunn	4002	£45.00
30/09/2010	7	HAS004	Haslam	4000	£12.00

All amounts in the table are **exclusive** of VAT at 20%

> **New Customer Details**
>
> Mr A Smith
> 12 Main Street
> Miltonby
> Lancashire
> LN87 4DF
>
> A/c Ref SMI009
>
> Credit terms: Payment in 14 days
>
> Credit Limit: £1000.00

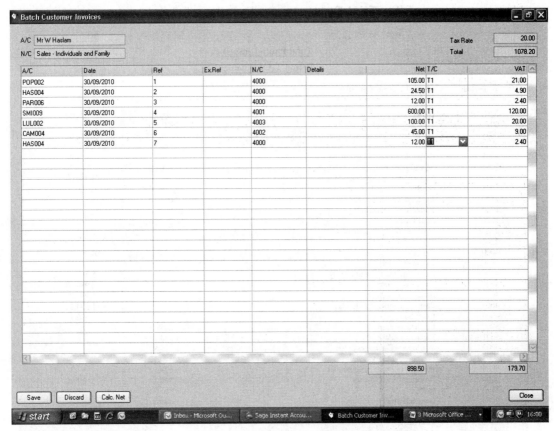

When you have entered all seven invoices, your screen should look like this. Check for accuracy, and when you are happy press the

Save button.

Now print out another Trial Balance for September 2010. Compare the two reports and identify the changes that have occurred.

Here is a copy of the Trial Balance produced earlier.

| Date: | 02/07/2012 | **Total Photo Limited** | | | Page: | 1 |
| Time: | 12:24:36 | **Period Trial Balance** | | | | |

To Period: Month 12, September 2010

N/C	Name	Debit	Credit
0022	Photographic Equipment	22,718.00	
0023	Depreciation (Photo Equipment)		4,316.00
0030	Office Equipment	4,849.00	
0031	Office Equipment Depreciation		921.00
0050	Motor Vehicles	21,800.00	
0051	Motor Vehicles Depreciation		5,450.00
1001	Stock	7,403.00	
1100	Debtors Control Account	4,053.10	
1200	Bank Current Account	10,293.00	
1230	Petty Cash	250.00	
2100	Creditors Control Account		19,192.41
2202	VAT Liability		1,623.29
3000	Capital		20,000.00
3200	Retained profits		5,498.28
4000	Sales - Individuals and Family		5,401.21
4001	Sales - Weddings		3,984.50
4002	Sales - Corporate		1,932.09
4003	Sales - Nurseries & Schools		11,304.20
4004	Other Sales		1,590.30
5000	Purchases - Film	205.63	
5001	Purchases - Paper	1,034.35	
5002	Purchases - Cartridges & toner	1,225.87	
5003	Purchases - Stationery	409.35	
5004	Purchases - Other consumables	823.52	
6900	Miscellaneous Expenses	229.39	
7100	Rent	3,800.00	
7103	General Rates	480.00	
7304	Miscellaneous Motor Expenses	1,035.64	
7502	Telephone	603.43	
	Totals:	**81,213.28**	**81,213.28**

Date: 26/06/2012   **Total Photo Limited**   Page: 1
Time: 14:48:09   **Period Trial Balance**

To Period: Month 12, September 2010

N/C	Name	Debit	Credit
0022	Photographic Equipment	22,718.00	
0023	Depreciation (Photo Equipment)		4,316.00
0030	Office Equipment	4,849.00	
0031	Office Equipment Depreciation		921.00
0050	Motor Vehicles	21,800.00	
0051	Motor Vehicles Depreciation		5,450.00
1001	Stock	7,403.00	
1100	Debtors Control Account	5,131.30 ❶	
1200	Bank Current Account	10,293.00	
1230	Petty Cash	250.00	
2100	Creditors Control Account		19,192.41
2200	Sales Tax Control Account		179.70
2202	VAT Liability		1,623.29 ❸
3000	Capital - Ordinary Shares		20,000.00
3200	Retained profits		5,498.28
4000	Sales - Individuals and Family		5,554.71
4001	Sales - Weddings		4,584.50
4002	Sales - Corporate		1,977.09
4003	Sales - Nurseries & Schools	❷	11,404.20
4004	Other Sales		1,590.30
5000	Purchases - Film	205.63	
5001	Purchases - Paper	1,034.35	
5002	Purchases - Cartridges & toner	1,225.87	
5003	Purchases - Stationery	409.35	
5004	Purchases - Other consumables	823.52	
6900	Miscellaneous Expenses	229.39	
7100	Rent	3,800.00	
7103	General Rates	480.00	
7304	Miscellaneous Motor Expenses	1,035.64	
7502	Telephone	603.43	
	Totals:	82,291.48	82,291.48

Notice which figures have changed.

(1) N/C 1100 (Debtors control account) has increased from £4053.10 to £5108.85. This reflects the fact that TotalPhoto Ltd is now owed an additional £1055.75 by its debtors.

(2) N/Cs 4000, 4001, 4002 and 4003 have increased, representing the new sales that the company made on 30th September. Note that the increase in these figures (£898.50) is the **net** increase in sales.

(3) There is a new Nominal Code (2200) called 'Sales Tax Control Account'. This control account automatically records all input VAT (on purchases) and output VAT (on sales) and is used to calculate and produce the company's VAT Return. The amount on this code is currently £179.70 (a **credit** balance) – the VAT charged on all the sales invoices you have entered.

3 Producing credit notes

A credit note is essentially a 'negative invoice' and is produced and sent to customers when a refund of money is needed. The most likely time this will happen is when goods that the organization has sold to a customer have been returned as faulty. They can also be used to correct errors etc.

Producing a credit note in SAGE is straightforward and effectively mirrors the process for producing an invoice.

Let us suppose that the sale of a 6" × 4" colour print made by TotalPhoto Ltd to Mr Pargenter for £12.00 (plus VAT) (Invoice No 3) is returned as faulty. It will be necessary to issue a credit note so that this debt is effectively 'removed' from Mr Pargenter's account.

From the **CUSTOMER** module select **CUSTOMER LIST** and then from the

icons at the top of the screen select the icon.

Here you can enter a batch of Credit Notes (just as you did with the batched invoices). SAGE shows your entries in RED to make it obvious that this is a Credit Note

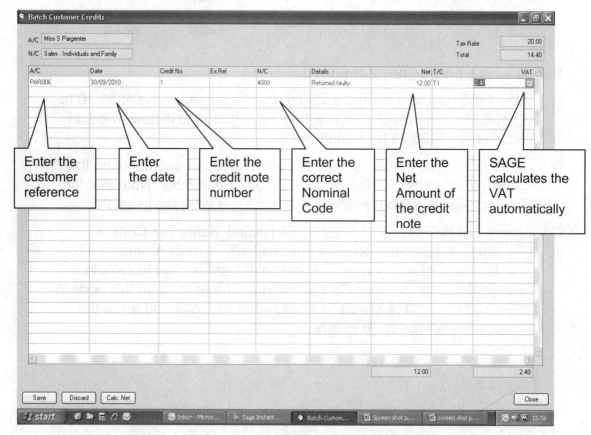

When you have entered all Credit Notes in the batch, and checked their accuracy, **SAVE** them to ensure that SAGE can process them.

4 Producing customer statements

Having produced and sent statements to customers, most businesses will also need to send periodic (usually monthly) statements to their customers which will list all new transactions – such as new purchases, payments received, credit notes issued etc.

SAGE allows the easy creation and production of customer statements.

Firstly, from the **CUSTOMER** module, press the  button.

This provides a choice of different statement layouts. You should use the one which best suits your business needs; however, for the purposes of this manual you should use the one called 'A4 Stat with Tear off Remit. Adv. Grouped & All Items'. Select this one by double-clicking.

In the **CRITERIA** screen (see below) use the pull-down menus to select customer Haslam (Ref HAS004). You can use the 'From...to...' feature to select a range of customers – but for now just select the one.

Make sure the Transaction dates are '01/09/2010' to '30/09/2010' – this will ensure that all transactions in September are shown.

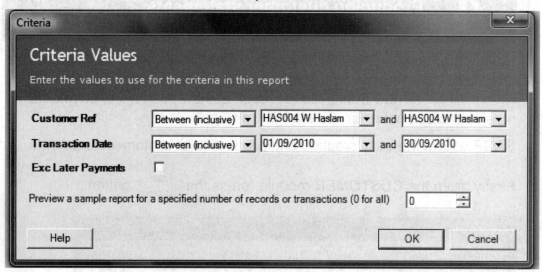

Press [OK] to create the report.

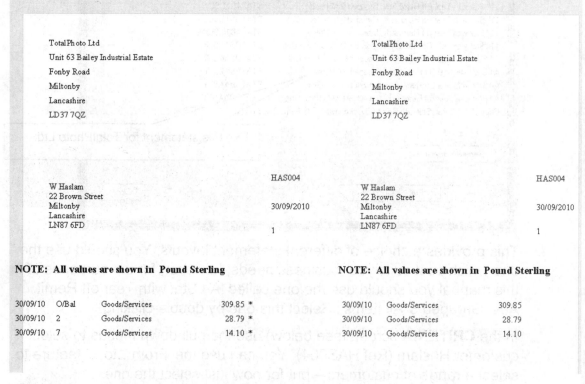

This statement could then be printed out (using special stationery if required) and then sent to suppliers.

Exercise

Create and print a customer statement for Mr Pargenter (Ref PAR006)

It should look like this:

Total Photo Limited
Unit 63 Bailey Industrial Estate
Fornby Road
Miltonby
Lancashire
LD37 7QZ

Miss S Pargenter
11 Alexandra Park

PAR006

30/09/2010

Miltonby
Lancashire
LN87 2WD

1

NOTE: All values are shown in Pound Sterling

| 30/09/10 | | Goods/Services | 650.00 * |
| 30/09/10 | 3 | Goods/Services | 14.40 * |

5 Credit purchases

When an organization purchases goods or services on credit, it will receive an invoice from the supplier. These must be recorded immediately in SAGE, even though they may not be paid for some time.

The most common way to process supplier invoices is to *batch* them (in much the same way as you did with the invoices to customers). This way, a number of invoices can be processed at the same time.

The process for entering batches of supplier statements is very similar to that for entering batches of customer invoices – except it is accessed via the **SUPPLIERS** module.

You should enter the **SUPPLIERS** module now.

Press the 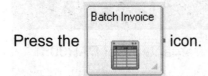 icon.

TotalPhoto Ltd received the following five invoices on 30th September 2010.

Invoice Ref	Supplier	Account	Net amount	Nominal Code
1341	Mackay Films	MF001	£208.76	5000
209	The Stationery Cupboard	SC003	£14.65	5003
216	The Stationery Cupboard	SC003	£78.92	5003
2203	Octopus Inks Ltd	OI001	£309.28	5002
10092	Mills Paper Products	MP002	£162.52	5001

You should now enter the above five supplier invoices as a batch.

When you have done this the screen should look like this:

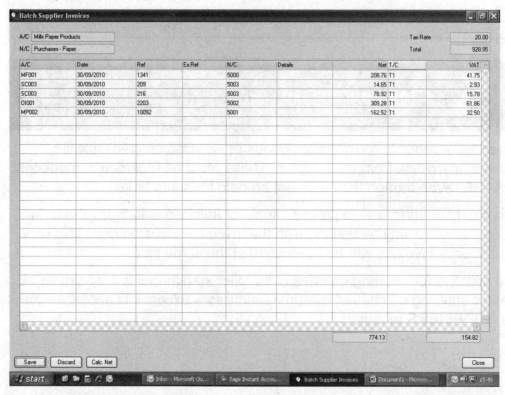

You should verify the entries and then press the **SAVE** button to post your entries to SAGE.

6 Supplier credit notes

These are processed in exactly the same way as you processed credit notes issued to customers.

Access the entry screen from the **SUPPLIERS** module.

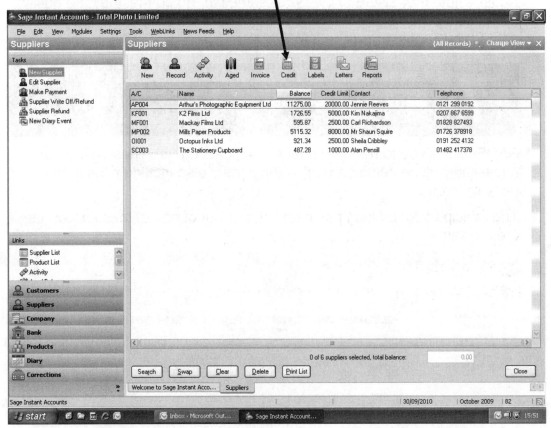

TotalPhoto Ltd receives one credit note. It is from Arthur's Photographic Equipment Ltd (Ref AP004) and is a credit for £2,109.99 (excluding VAT) for a camera that was returned as faulty. The credit note reference is 134C. The Nominal Code for this is 0022 (Fixed Asset – Photographic Equipment).

You should enter this as follows:

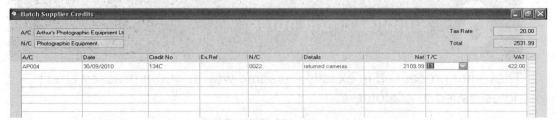

Again – note that SAGE shows your entries in red so that they are easily identifiable as a credit note. When you have checked the accuracy of your entries you should press the **SAVE** button.

7 Bank transactions

SAGE allows you to run a number of 'bank accounts'. These need not necessarily all be held at a bank – they could also include cash in hand, petty cash etc.

The principles for making payments into or out of any of these accounts are the same.

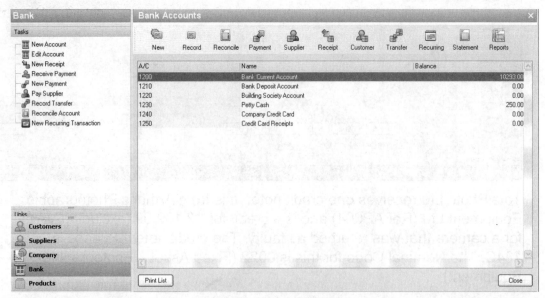

Enter the **Bank** module. You can see that SAGE has already set up a number of different bank accounts, each with its own Nominal Code. You can of course amend these or add to them if you wish.

The most commonly used bank account is probably Nominal Code 1200. This is the one that you will use in this manual for payments into and out of TotalPhoto Ltd's main current bank account. You can see that it has a balance at the moment of £10,293.00. You may recall that this was the opening balance that you entered earlier. None of the entries that you have made since then have affected the bank balance.

8 Making payments

TotalPhoto Ltd has three payments to make on 30th September 2010. These are:

- A cheque for £107.65 (plus VAT at 20.0%) to Arrow Telecoms to pay the telephone bill

- A cheque for £55.00 to Miltonby Cricket Association for advertising in their League Handbook (no VAT on this transaction)

- A cheque for £45.00 to Miltonby Borough Council for a parking permit (no VAT)

To enter these transactions click the button.

Enter each transaction as a separate line. Be careful to make sure you select the appropriate Nominal Code for the expense item, and also the correct VAT rate. Your entries should look like this:

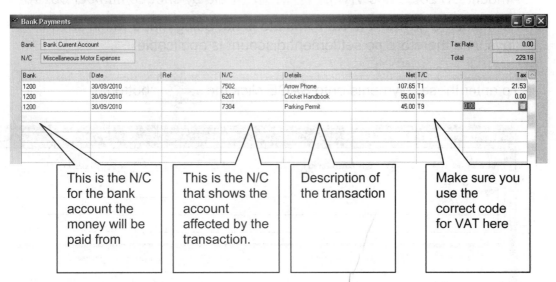

When you have checked your entries, **SAVE** them to SAGE.

Now check the balance on Nominal Code 1200 (the bank current account).

See how the bank balance has now gone down to £10066.51 – reflecting the fact that payments of £229.18 (£207.65 plus £21.53 VAT) have been taken from it.

Paying Suppliers

TotalPhoto Ltd also decides to pay two outstanding creditors on 30th September, as follows:

The Stationery Cupboard (SC003)
Amount: £375 inc VAT   *Paid by cheque number 00245*

K2 Films Ltd (KF001)
Amount £1726.55 (inc VAT).   *Paid by cheque number 00246*

Note that the payment to K2 Films Ltd is not being made within seven days, and therefore no settlement discount is applicable.

To enter these payments onto SAGE click the  button.

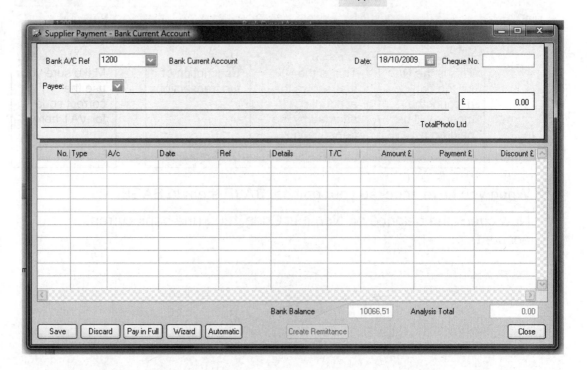

Use the drop down menu to select the first supplier to pay – in this The Stationery Cupboard. Enter the correct date, the cheque number and the amount being paid (£375.00).

Note how SAGE has completed the bottom half of the screen with the outstanding invoices for this supplier. This allows you to decide which outstanding invoices you want to pay.

Enter £375.00 against the opening balance amount – this is the invoice being paid on this occasion.

Note that SAGE can automatically decide which invoices to pay, or, if you wish to pay all outstanding invoices, you can select to Pay in Full

Save your payment.

Now enter the next payment, to K2 Films Ltd, in the same way.

9 Recording receipts

The most likely sources of receipts for most businesses are:

- Cash Sales

- Receipts from Debtors

You will look at these in turn.

Cash Sales

TotalPhoto Ltd also sells items to two customers who pay cash on 30th September. The first of these is a 6" × 4" Colour Print for £12.00 plus VAT; the second is for School Photos (Set 2) for £28.00 plus VAT.

TotalPhoto Ltd has decided to open a new 'bank' account called 'Cash in Hand'. This will be used to record the payments into and out of the cash register.

Firstly, you will need to set up this new account, using the N/C 1225.

Click the icon from the **BANK** module.

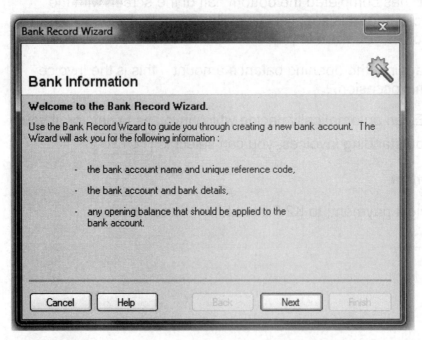

Click **NEXT.**

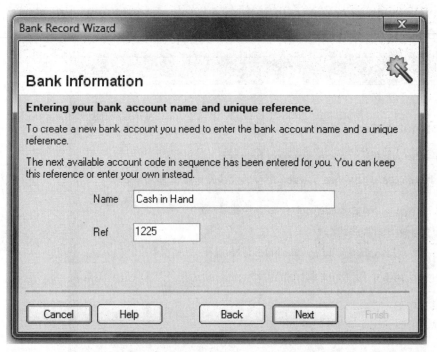

On this screen, change the details to "Cash In Hand" and "1225" and then click **next.**

Set this account as a "Cash Account" using the drop down menu, then click **next.**

Because this is a cash account, rather than a bank account, you can skip the next three screens, until you get to this one:

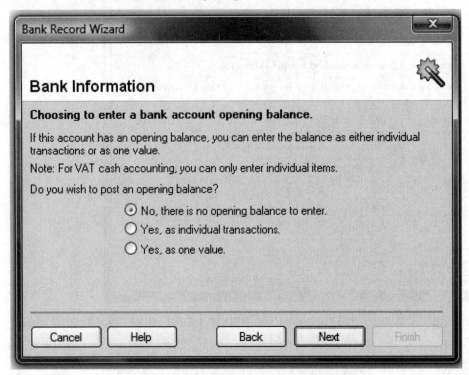

This time, there is no opening balance. Click **Next** to complete setting up this new account.

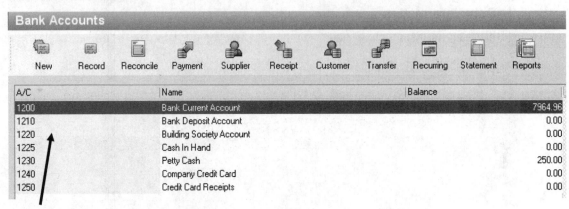

Note the new account you have just set up.

Use the 'blue bar' to highlight code 1225 then click the icon.

Enter the two cash sales as below:

Enter the appropriate N/C for the type of receipt – here, N/C 4000 is 'Sales – Individual and Family'

This is for the tax code – here, T1 in both cases

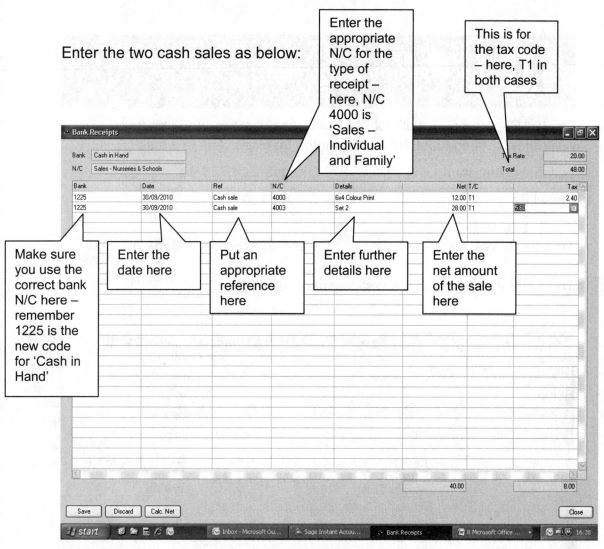

Make sure you use the correct bank N/C here – remember 1225 is the new code for 'Cash in Hand'

Enter the date here

Put an appropriate reference here

Enter further details here

Enter the net amount of the sale here

When you have entered both transactions press **SAVE**.

You should now see that there is a balance on N/C 1225 of £48.00 – the total amount of the two cash sales.

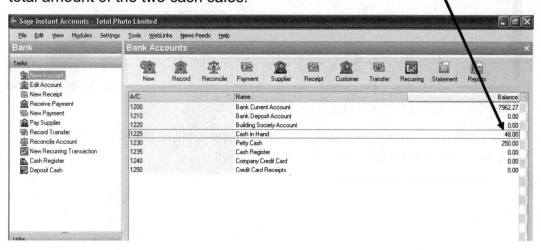

10 Receipts from customers

On 30th September TotalPhoto Ltd also received two amounts from customers in respect of their outstanding invoices. These were:

Lullabies Nursery (LUL002)   Cheque for £726.90

Mrs H Poppy   Cash £120.00

To enter these, firstly click the icon from with the **Bank** module.

The enter the details of the first payment as follows.

> Be sure to use the correct Bank Account

> Enter the amount of the cheque received

> Allocate the receipt against the relevant outstanding invoice

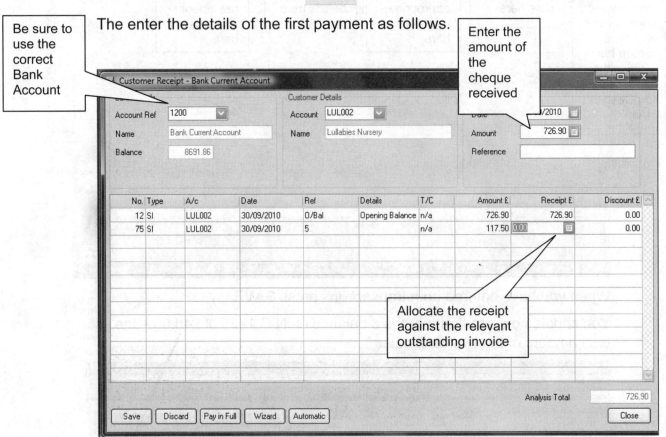

Click **Save** to post this entry to SAGE.

Now enter the second receipt, from Mrs Poppy. Note that only £120.00 has been received, and that she paid in cash.

Your screen should look like this:

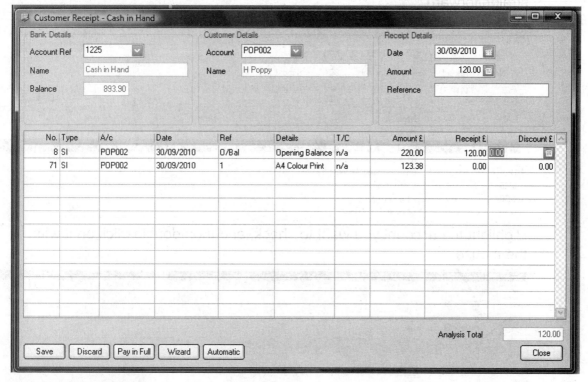

Again, click on **Save.**

When recording BACS receipts the same process should be followed however the date that the amount is received in the bank should be recorded as the date and the reference should generally be the name of the supplier so it ties in what appears with what is on the bank receipt. This makes it easier to perform the bank reconciliation (see later on in the manual).

11 Checking bank activity

It is important for businesses to regularly check their bank transactions. There are a number of reasons for this:

- To monitor the bank balance to ensure that there is sufficient money to meet liabilities

- To monitor transactions to ensure against fraud or theft

- To ensure there is not too much money in any particular account. For example, if the balance in the current account reaches a certain level the business may decide to transfer some of it to a different account where it may earn a higher rate of interest.

Checking the activity on any Nominal Code (not just for the bank) is straightforward.

Highlight the account you want to check, and then double-click on it with the mouse.

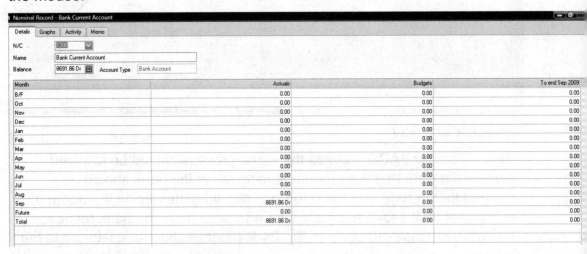

Choose the Activity tab at the top.

You should now see the following screen.

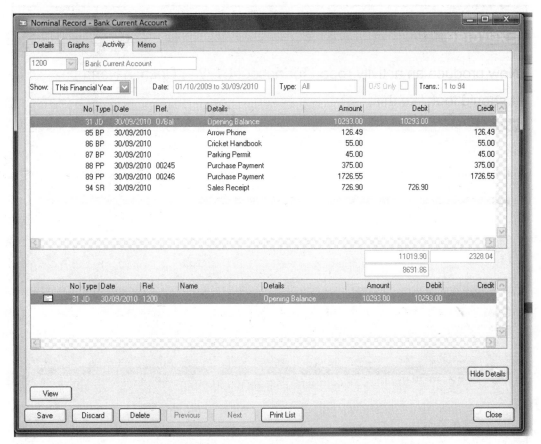

This shows all the transactions to date affecting N/C 1200 (the main current account). Make sure you can identify all of these.

Note that Debit entries represent monies paid **into** the bank account; credit entries show payments **out of** the bank account.

Exercise

Now produce an activity report for account 1225 ('Cash in Hand')

It should look like this:

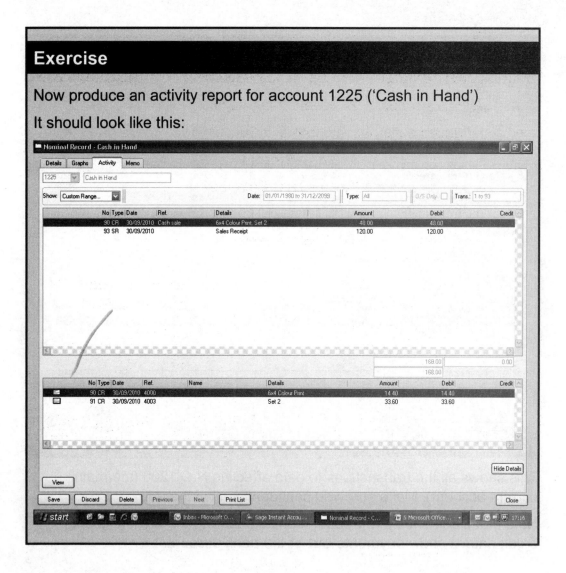

Exercise

You should now produce a revised Trial Balance.

Your Trial Balance should now look like this.

TotalPhotoLtd

Period Trial Balance

Date: 26/06/2012	**Total Photo Limited**	**Page:** 1
Time: 17:22:01	**Period Trial Balance**	

To Period: Month 12, September 2010

N/C	Name	Debit	Credit
0022	Photographic Equipment	20,608.01	
0023	Depreciation (Photo Equipment)		4,316.00
0030	Office Equipment	4,849.00	
0031	Office Equipment Depreciation		921.00
0050	Motor Vehicles	21,800.00	
0051	Motor Vehicles Depreciation		5,450.00
1001	Stock	7,403.00	
1100	Debtors Control Account	4,270.00	
1200	Bank Current Account	8,689.17	
1225	Cash in Hand	168.00	
1230	Petty Cash	250.00	
2100	Creditors Control Account		15,487.82
2200	Sales Tax Control Account		185.30
2201	Purchase Tax Control Account		245.65
2202	VAT Liability		1,623.29
3000	Capital - Ordinary Shares		20,000.00
3200	Retained profits		5,498.28
4000	Sales - Individuals and Family		5,554.71
4001	Sales - Weddings		4,584.50
4002	Sales - Corporate		1,977.09
4003	Sales - Nurseries & Schools		11,432.20
4004	Other Sales		1,590.30
5000	Purchases - Film	414.39	
5001	Purchases - Paper	1,196.87	
5002	Purchases - Cartridges & toner	1,535.15	
5003	Purchases - Stationery	502.92	
5004	Purchases - Other consumables	823.52	
6201	Advertising	55.00	
6900	Miscellaneous Expenses	229.39	
7100	Rent	3,800.00	
7103	General Rates	480.00	
7304	Miscellaneous Motor Expenses	1,080.64	
7502	Telephone	711.08	
	Totals:	78,866.14	78,866.14

12 Transfers

Sometimes a business may transfer money from one account to another. For example, it may transfer money from 'Cash in Hand' to the 'Current Bank Account'. Alternatively, it may transfer an amount from the current account to a deposit account. It may also need to reimburse the petty cash account with money from the current account or cash in hand.

From the **Bank** module click the  icon.

TotalPhoto Ltd operates a petty cash tin, to be used for items such as stamps, milk, tea, coffee, taxi fares etc.

It operates an *IMPREST* system, with an imprest amount of £250.00. However, it decides that this is too high an amount and so decides to reduce the imprest amount to £100. It therefore takes £150 from the tin and banks it in the current account.

You should enter the details of this transfer as below and then **Save.**

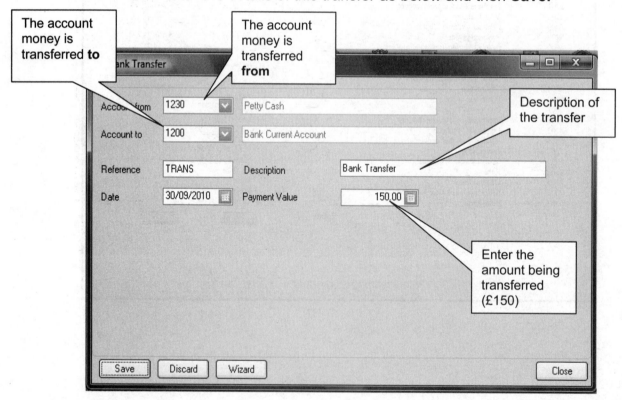

13 Petty cash

Most businesses use petty cash as a way of paying for minor expenses such as taxi fares, tea, milk and coffee, window cleaning etc. We have already seen that TotalPhoto Ltd operate a petty cash tin with an imprest amount of £100.

Payments out of petty cash are recorded in exactly the same way as any other payments made from a bank account. Remember to make sure that you use the correct account number (1230).

Also be sure to enter the correct VAT code for each transaction. Many items commonly paid for out of petty cash are zero-rated or exempt – but not all.

TotalPhoto Ltd makes the following payments out of petty cash on 30th September 2010.

Voucher No	Description	Amount	VAT?
11762	Window cleaner	£4.00	No
11763	Tea and milk	£2.65	No
11764	Newspapers	£3.00	No
11765	Stamps	£3.60	No
11766	Pens	£1.99	Inclusive at 20.0%
11767	Taxi fare	£8.00	No

Enter these by clicking on the button.

Make sure that the account selected is 1230 – petty cash.

Enter each of the transactions above.

Your screen should look like this:

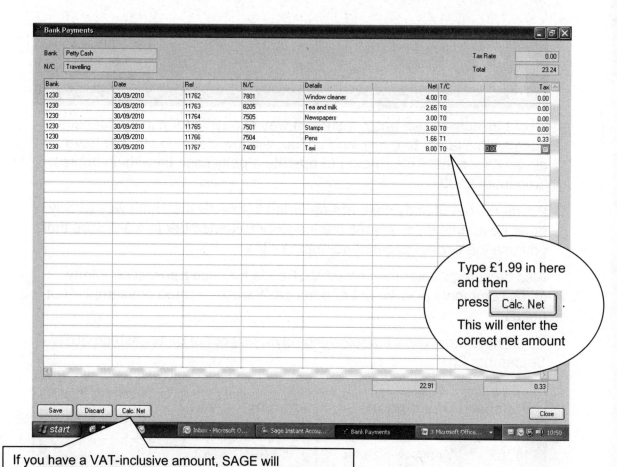

If you have a VAT-inclusive amount, SAGE will automatically calculate the VAT element for you. Simply type the gross amount in the box and press this button, or press F9.

Once you have verified this click **Save.**

Reimbursing the Petty Cash Account

To reimburse the petty cash account, simply transfer the money from one account (usually the current account or cash in hand) to the petty cash account.

TotalPhoto Ltd reimbursed their petty cash tin at the end of 30th September with the amount necessary to bring the float back to £100.00. The amount spent during the day was £23.24 and so this is the amount to be reimbursed. This money was taken from the 'Cash in Hand' account.

The transfer entry should look like this:

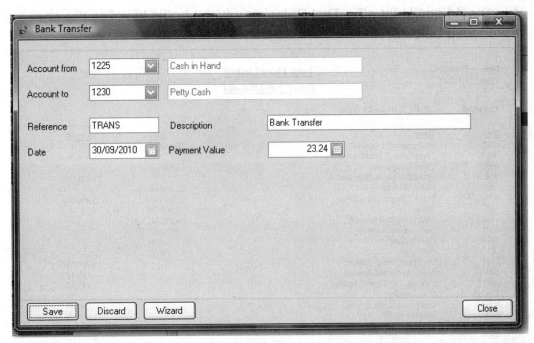

You should now also see that the balance on the petty cash account has been restored to £100, whilst the balance of cash in hand is now £143.76.

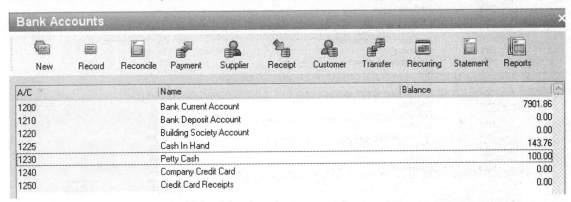

You have now learnt how to process the vast majority of transactions that most businesses will deal with on a day to day basis.

You should now print off a Trial Balance, which should look like the one reproduced below.

Date:	27/06/2012	**Total Photo Limited**	Page:	1
Time:	11:10:41	**Period Trial Balance**		

To Period: Month 12, September 2010

N/C	Name	Debit	Credit
0022	Photographic Equipment	20,608.01	
0023	Depreciation (Photo Equipment)		4,316.00
0030	Office Equipment	4,849.00	
0031	Office Equipment Depreciation		921.00
0050	Motor Vehicles	21,800.00	
0051	Motor Vehicles Depreciation		5,450.00
1001	Stock	7,403.00	
1100	Debtors Control Account	4,270.00	
1200	Bank Current Account	8,839.17	
1225	Cash in Hand	144.76	
1230	Petty Cash	100.00	
2100	Creditors Control Account		15,487.82
2200	Sales Tax Control Account		185.30
2201	Purchase Tax Control Account		245.32
2202	VAT Liability		1,623.29
3000	Capital - Ordinary Shares		20,000.00
3200	Retained profits		5,498.28
4000	Sales - Individuals and Family		5,554.71
4001	Sales - Weddings		4,584.50
4002	Sales - Corporate		1,977.09
4003	Sales - Nurseries & Schools		11,432.20
4004	Other Sales		1,590.30
5000	Purchases - Film	414.39	
5001	Purchases - Paper	1,196.87	
5002	Purchases - Cartridges & toner	1,535.15	
5003	Purchases - Stationery	502.92	
5004	Purchases - Other consumables	823.52	
6201	Advertising	55.00	
6900	Miscellaneous Expenses	229.39	
7100	Rent	3,800.00	
7103	General Rates	480.00	
7304	Miscellaneous Motor Expenses	1,080.64	
7400	Travelling	8.00	
7501	Postage and Carriage	3.60	
7502	Telephone	711.08	
7504	Office Stationery	1.66	
7505	Books etc.	3.00	
7801	Cleaning	4.00	
8205	Refreshments	2.65	
	Totals:	78,865.81	78,865.81

Journals

9

KNOWLEDGE

2.1 Select and use appropriate tools and techniques to enter and process transactions

2.2 Review transaction process and identify any errors

2.3 Respond appropriately to any transaction errors and problems

2.4 Select and use appropriate tools and techniques to process period end routines

CONTENTS

1 Introduction

2 Correction of errors

3 Bad debts

1 Introduction

So far you have learnt how to process day-to-day transactions through SAGE. These have included making sales and purchases and making and receiving payments.

Sometimes, however, a business will need to record an accounting transaction that falls outside the 'norm'. In these instances, a *journal* is required.

Common reasons for journals

- **Correction of errors – for example, amending opening balances, removing duplicate entries, or correcting given or your own errors**

- **Writing off bad debts**

- **Year end adjustments (e.g. depreciation, accruals and prepayments, closing stock). *You do not need to be aware of this for this assessment.***

2 Correction of errors

You may find that you enter a transaction incorrectly, and post it to SAGE before you have noticed. In this instance you will need to correct the error by producing a reversing journal.

Earlier, you entered a payment from the bank for £55.00 to Miltonby Cricket Association for advertising in their handbook.

It has now come to light that in fact the payment should have been for £85.00, the error being due to misreading the League Secretary's rather poor handwriting on the invoice. The correct amount was in fact paid – reference to the cheque stub and the bank statement would confirm this.

The problem

At the moment, the bank balance is overstated by £30, as we have only entered £55 instead of the correct amount of £85. Also, the expenditure on advertising is understated by the same £30.

The solution

You need to produce a journal to correct this error.

From the **Company** module select the icon.

Enter the details as below:

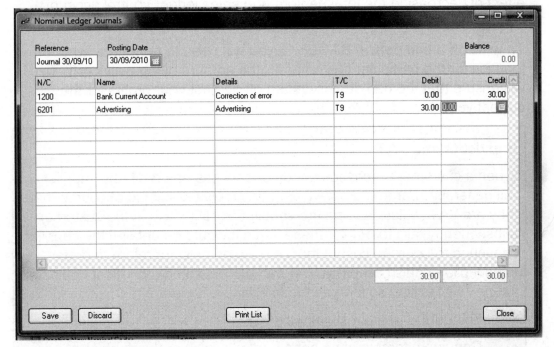

Note the double-entry:

You have credited the bank account by £30 and debited the advertising account by the same amount.

If you need to learn more about double entry bookkeeping refer to your manual bookkeeping textbook.

Press **Save.**

3 Bad debts

A bad debt arises when a debtor fails to make payment on their debt to us. At some point the organization will need to judge that the debt is no longer likely to be recovered and will need to write off the debt. This has the effect of decreasing the total debtors (the sales ledger control account) and creating a bad debt expense that will reduce profits.

To write off a bad debt in SAGE v16 you will need to perform a 'write off' function for the particular customer for the amount being written off. This will ensure that the bad debt is written off against your profits for the current year.

Bad debts and VAT

When a customer purchases goods or services on credit, the supplier will generally charge them VAT on that supply (assuming of course that they are VAT registered and the supplies attract VAT). If the customer subsequently fails to pay for these items it would be unfair if the supplier continued to bear the cost of the VAT. Rules exist therefore to protect the supplier in this case. The VAT can be reclaimed (i.e. offset against a future VAT liability) so long as the following criteria are met:

- The debt is at least six months old

- Genuine attempts have been made to recover the debt

- The debt has been written off in the accounts

TotalPhoto Ltd is currently showing as a debtor T Pashby (A/c Ref PAS002). This debt relates to photographs sold almost a year ago. A number of letters have been sent to the given address but have been returned as 'not living at this address anymore'. Attempts to telephone the customer have proved equally as fruitless.

A decision has now been taken to write off the bad debt (£89.50 including VAT).

This is processed as follows:

From within the **CORRECTIONS** module, click on 'Cust write off/refund' as shown below:

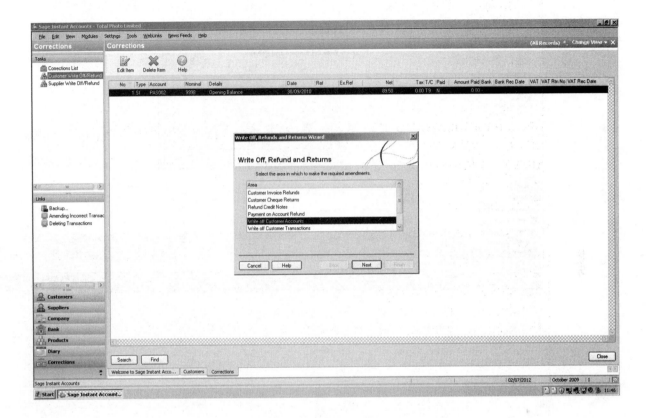

Click on 'write off customer accounts', then select the customer
(Mrs T Pashby). Proceed through the screens, entering 'Bad debt write off'
as the additional reference. Check the details are correct before clicking
'finish'. See the screen shot on the next page.

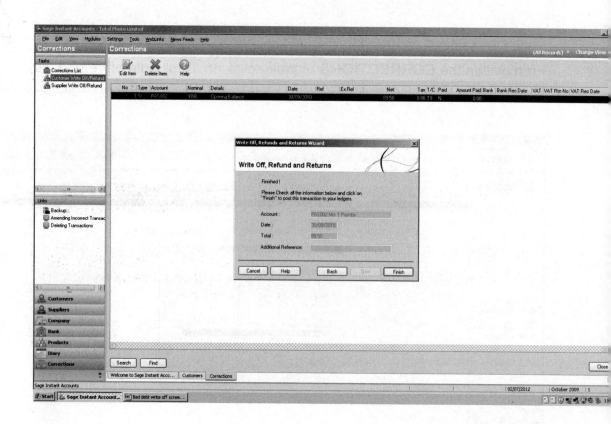

Bank reconciliation

1 Introduction

A useful exercise for all businesses to undertake on a regular basis is to reconcile their bank account. In essence this means checking the company's own records with the bank statement produced and sent to them by their bank.

TotalPhoto Ltd received the following statement from their bank.

STATEMENT			
Account number			
Sort code			
Date	Payments	Receipts	Balance
30/09/10 Op Bal			10293.00
30/09/10 Lodgement		150.00	10443.00
30/09/10 Interest		11.22	10454.22
30/09/10 Bank Charges	31.41		10422.81
30/09/10 DD North West Radio	240.00		10182.81
03/10/10 Chq 242	85.00		10097.81

The bank statement will rarely agree exactly with the company's own records, for three reasons:

1 **Items on the Bank Statement not yet recorded in SAGE**

There may be some items on the bank statement which do not yet appear in the company's records. Here, there is interest which has been credited to the business' account of £11.22, and also bank charges of £31.41 which have been debited from the account. There is also a direct debit for £240.00 It is likely that the company would not know the exact amount or date of these receipts to/payments from the bank account until the statement is actually received. Similarly, you should always check that all standing orders/ direct debits / BACS transfers etc have been fully recorded in the company's records. Remember that a 'recurring item' can be set up within SAGE but that these must still be posted.

Discrepancies between the bank statement and the company's own records of this nature should be dealt with by updating the company's records.

You should now produce enter a **bank payment** to deal with the bank charges and the direct debit, and a **bank receipt** to deal with the interest received.

Here is the screen for the **bank payments.** Remember there is no VAT on bank charges (or interest) and so the VAT code should be set to T9.

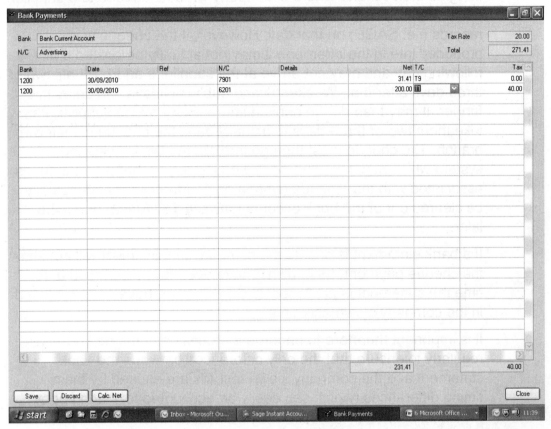

And here is the screen for the **bank receipt** of the interest. Note that there was no Nominal Code for *Bank Interest Received* and so a new N/C has been created (N/C 4906).

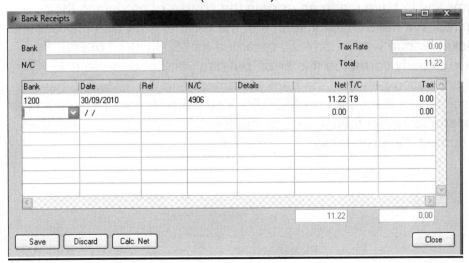

2   **Timing Differences**

This is a very common cause of discrepancies between the bank statement and the company's own records. Timing differences occur because the company will generally update its records before the bank has had the opportunity to process all transactions.

Imagine the scenario where a company writes a cheque to a supplier on 1st March. The accounts clerk is likely to update the company's records (i.e. SAGE) on that day. However, if the cheque was produced late in the afternoon it may not actually be posted until the following day and may not arrive at the supplier's address until two or three days after that. Weekends and public holidays can delay this further. It may then not be banked immediately by the supplier; it may take them two or three days to actually bank the cheque in their own branch. The cheque must then go through the banks' clearing system which may take three-five working days. Therefore the funds associated with that cheque (written on 1st March) may not actually be cleared out of the bank account until say 10th March or maybe later.

If a bank statement is sent to the company in this time it will not show the cheque payment, as it will not have been fully processed at the time the statement is produced. It will, however, have been recorded in the company's own accounts.

It is important therefore to undergo a process of bank reconciliation regularly to ensure that the only differences between the bank statement and the company's own records are caused by these timing differences (which can easily be accounted for), and not by the third reason for discrepancies, which is error.

3   **Errors**

It is perfectly possible for either the bank or (more likely) the company to have made an error in the course of producing their figures. We have already seen that the payment hat was made to the cricket league was incorrectly recorded as £55 instead of £85. You have already corrected this error, but had you not done so the reconciliation between the bank statement and SAGE would have resulted in a discrepancy of £30.00. You would therefore have had to undertake further investigations into the cause of the error and then to correct it appropriately.

2 Performing a bank reconciliation using SAGE

From the **BANK** Module click on the 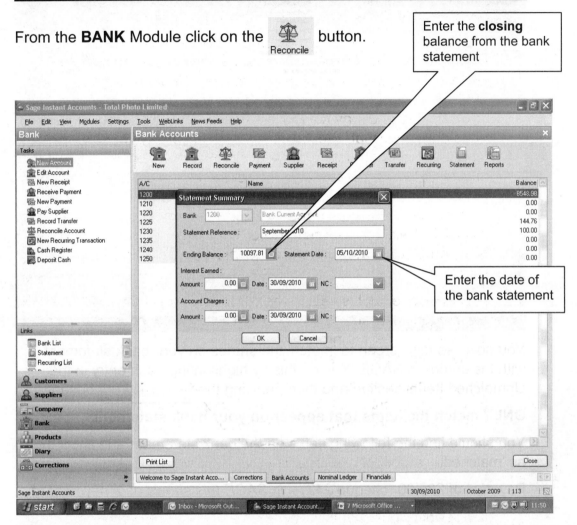 button.

Enter the **closing** balance from the bank statement

Enter the date of the bank statement

This screen allows you to enter the summary of your Bank Statement. Notice that you can also enter the interest earned and any bank charges directly via this screen as well (rather than entering them separately as bank payments and receipts as you did earlier).

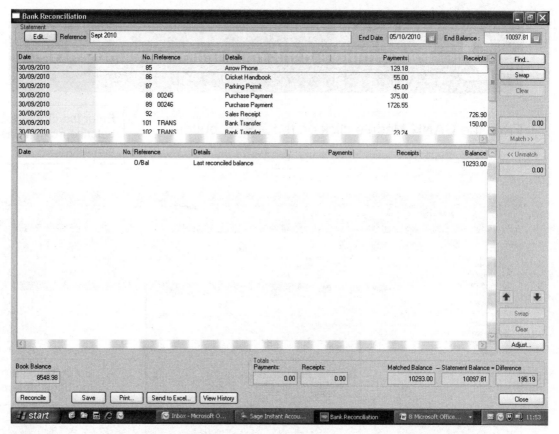

You now use this screen to 'match' the entries on your bank statement with the entries in SAGE. You do this by highlighting each entry in the Unmatched Items section and then pressing the [Match >>] button.

ONLY match the items that appear on your bank statement

You should find the following items on the bank statement and show them as 'matched'

Payment of £85.00 (cheque 242) – *in SAGE this shows as a payment of £55.00 and a journal entry of £30.00; you should 'match' both of these items.*

Lodgement of £150.00

Bank interest of £11.22

Bank charges of £31.41

Direct Debit to North West Radios of £240.00

Once you have matched all items they will appear in the 'Matched Against Statement' box as shown below:

You can see here that the items which appear on the bank statement have now been matched. The matched balance now equals the statement balance and there is now therefore no difference.

You should now press the Reconcile button to complete the process.

3 Reports

Once you have reconciled the bank statement you should produce the following reports from within the **BANK – REPORTS** module:

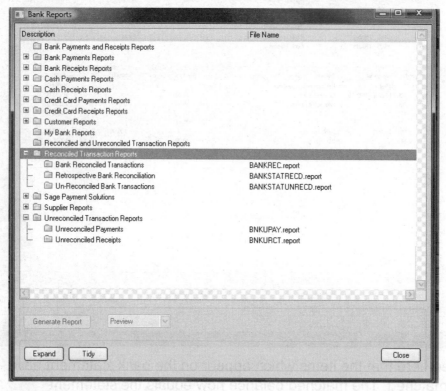

BANKREC.report shows the list of matched and reconciled items within SAGE.

BNKUPAY.srt shows the list of unreconciled payments – these are the payments that you have recorded in SAGE but which do not yet appear on the latest bank statement.

BNKURCT.srt shows the list or unreconciled receipts – again, these are receipts which do not yet appear on the bank statement.

You should produce and print each of these reports now.

KAPLAN PUBLISHING

BANKREC.report

| Date: | 27/06/2012 | | | | | **Total Photo Limited** | | | | Page: | 1 |
| Time: | 12:15:10 | | | | | **Bank Reconciled Transactions** | | | | | |

Bank Reconciled On: 30/09/2010

No	Type	Date	A/C	N/C	Dept	Ref	Details	Net	Tax	T/C
36	JD	30/09/2010	1200	1200	0	O/Bal	Opening Balance	10,293.00	0.00	T9

Bank Reconciled On: 05/10/2010

No	Type	Date	A/C	N/C	Dept	Ref	Details	Net	Tax	T/C
86	BP	30/09/2010	1200	6201	0		Cricket Handbook	55.00	0.00	T9
101	JD	30/09/2010	1200	1200	0	TRANS	Bank Transfer	150.00	0.00	T9
108	JC	30/09/2010	1200	1200	0	Journal	Correction of error	30.00	0.00	T9
111	BP	30/09/2010	1200	7901	0			31.41	0.00	T9
112	BR	30/09/2010	1200	4906	0			11.22	0.00	T9
113	BP	30/09/2010	1200	6201	0		DD	200.00	40.00	T1

BNKUPAY.report

| Date: | 27/06/2012 | **Total Photo Limited** | Page: | 1 |
| Time: | 12:16:33 | **Unreconciled Payments** | | |

| Date From: | 01/01/1980 | Bank From: | 1200 |
| DateTo: | 31/12/2019 | Bank To: | 1200 |

| Transaction From: | 1 |
| Transaction To: | 99,999,999 |

Bank	1200		Bank Account Name	Bank Current Account		Currency	Pound Sterling	
No	Type	Date	Ref	Details			Amount	£
85	BP	30/09/2010		Arrow Phone			129.18	
87	BP	30/09/2010		Parking Permit			45.00	
88	PP	30/09/2010	00245	Purchase Payment			375.00	
89	PP	30/09/2010	00246	Purchase Payment			1,726.55	
102	JC	30/09/2010	TRANS	Bank Transfer			23.24	
						Total £	2,298.97	

BNKURCT.srt

| Date: | 19/10/2009 | **TotalPhoto Ltd** | Page: | 1 |
| Time: | 20:08:46 | **Unreconciled Receipts** | | |

| Date From: | 01/01/1980 | BankFrom: | 1200 |
| DateTo: | 31/12/2019 | BankTo: | 1200 |

| Transaction From: | 1 |
| Transaction To: | 99,999,999 |

Bank	1200		Bank Account Name	Bank Current Account		Currency	Pound Sterling	
No	Type	Date	Ref	Details			Amount	£
94	SR	30/09/2010		Sales Receipt			726.90	
						Total £	726.90	

These payments and receipts will appear on future bank statements, when they will then be matched in a future reconciliation.

Useful reports

11

KNOWLEDGE

3.1 Describe what information is required and how to present it

3.2 Prepare and generate accounting documents

3.3 Prepare and generate management reports as required

CONTENTS

1 Introduction

Although it is possible to create and produce your own SAGE reports, there are a number of extremely useful report layouts already set up within SAGE.

You have already seen a number of these throughout the manual.

You should now make yourself familiar with these, plus the other reports shown below.

Note that there are many other reports within SAGE; you should take the time to examine all of these to find the reports that will best suit your business.

2 Customer reports

Aged Debtors Analysis (Report CSTAGED.report)

| Date: | 27/06/2012 | | **Total Photo Limited** | Page: | 1 |
| Time: | 12:22:07 | | **Aged Debtors Analysis (Detailed)** | | |

Date From:	01/01/1980		Customer From:	
Date To:	30/09/2010		Customer To:	ZZZZZZZZ
Include future transactions:	No			
Exclude later payments:	No			

** NOTE: All report values are shown in Base Currency, unless otherwise indicated **

A/C: CAM004   Name: Campbell & Dunn   Contact: Tel:

No	Type	Date	Ref	Details	Balance	Future	Current	Period 1	Period 2	Period 3	Older
11	SI	30/09/2010		Opening Balance	2,056.85	0.00	2,056.85	0.00	0.00	0.00	0.00
18	SI	30/09/2010	6		54.00	0.00	54.00	0.00	0.00	0.00	0.00
				Totals:	2,110.85	0.00	2,110.85	0.00	0.00	0.00	0.00

Turnover: 2,101.85
Credit Limit £ 2,500.00

A/C: HAS004   Name: Mr W Haslam   Contact: Tel:

No	Type	Date	Ref	Details	Balance	Future	Current	Period 1	Period 2	Period 3	Older
7	SI	30/09/2010		Opening Balance	309.85	0.00	309.85	0.00	0.00	0.00	0.00
14	SI	30/09/2010	2		29.40	0.00	29.40	0.00	0.00	0.00	0.00
19	SI	30/09/2010	7		14.40	0.00	14.40	0.00	0.00	0.00	0.00
				Totals:	353.65	0.00	353.65	0.00	0.00	0.00	0.00

Turnover: 346.35
Credit Limit £ 500.00

A/C: LUL002   Name: Lullabies Nursery   Contact: Tel:

No	Type	Date	Ref	Details	Balance	Future	Current	Period 1	Period 2	Period 3	Older
17	SI	30/09/2010	5		120.00	0.00	120.00	0.00	0.00	0.00	0.00
				Totals:	120.00	0.00	120.00	0.00	0.00	0.00	0.00

Turnover: 826.90
Credit Limit £ 1,500.00

A/C: PAR006   Name: Miss S Pargenter   Contact: Tel:

No	Type	Date	Ref	Details	Balance	Future	Current	Period 1	Period 2	Period 3	Older
9	SI	30/09/2010		Opening Balance	650.00	0.00	650.00	0.00	0.00	0.00	0.00
15	SI	30/09/2010	3		14.40	0.00	14.40	0.00	0.00	0.00	0.00
84	SC	30/09/2010	1	Returned faulty	-14.40	0.00	-14.40	0.00	0.00	0.00	0.00
				Totals:	650.00	0.00	650.00	0.00	0.00	0.00	0.00

Turnover: 650.00
Credit Limit £ 1,000.00

A/C: POP002   Name: Mrs H Poppy   Contact: Tel:

No	Type	Date	Ref	Details	Balance	Future	Current	Period 1	Period 2	Period 3	Older
8	SI	30/09/2010		Opening Balance	100.00	0.00	100.00	0.00	0.00	0.00	0.00
13	SI	30/09/2010	1		126.00	0.00	126.00	0.00	0.00	0.00	0.00
				Totals:	226.00	0.00	226.00	0.00	0.00	0.00	0.00

Turnover: 325.00
Credit Limit £ 500.00

A/C: SMI009   Name: Mr A Smith   Contact: Tel:

No	Type	Date	Ref	Details	Balance	Future	Current	Period 1	Period 2	Period 3	Older
16	SI	30/09/2010	4		720.00	0.00	720.00	0.00	0.00	0.00	0.00
				Totals:	720.00	0.00	720.00	0.00	0.00	0.00	0.00

Turnover: 600.00
Credit Limit £ 1,000.00

| | | | | Grand Totals: | 4,180.50 | 0.00 | 4,180.50 | 0.00 | 0.00 | 0.00 | 0.00 |

Shows a list of debtors with analysis of how long the debts have been in existence

Day Books – Customer Invoices (Report CSTDYIVD.report)

Date:	27/06/2012					**Total Photo Limited**			Page:	1		
Time:	12:19:49					**Day Books: Customer Invoices (Detailed)**						

Date From:	01/01/1980	Customer From:	
Date To:	31/12/2019	Customer To:	ZZZZZZZZ

Transaction From:	1	N/C From:	
Transaction To:	99,999,999	N/C To:	99999999

Dept From:	0
Dept To:	999

Tran No.	Type	Date	A/C Ref	N/C	Inv Ref	Dept.	Details	Net Amount	Tax Amount	T/C	Gross Amount	V	B
7	SI	30/09/2010	HAS004	9998		0	Opening Balance	309.85	0.00	T9	309.85	-	-
8	SI	30/09/2010	POP002	9998		0	Opening Balance	220.00	0.00	T9	220.00	-	-
9	SI	30/09/2010	PAR006	9998		0	Opening Balance	650.00	0.00	T9	650.00	-	-
10	SI	30/09/2010	PAS002	9998		0	Opening Balance	89.50	0.00	T9	89.50	-	-
11	SI	30/09/2010	CAM004	9998		0	Opening Balance	2,056.85	0.00	T9	2,056.85	-	-
12	SI	30/09/2010	LUL002	9998		0	Opening Balance	726.90	0.00	T9	726.90	-	-
13	SI	30/09/2010	POP002	4000	1	0		105.00	21.00	T1	126.00	N	-
14	SI	30/09/2010	HAS004	4000	2	0		24.50	4.90	T1	29.40	N	-
15	SI	30/09/2010	PAR006	4000	3	0		12.00	2.40	T1	14.40	N	-
16	SI	30/09/2010	SMI009	4001	4	0		600.00	120.00	T1	720.00	N	-
17	SI	30/09/2010	LUL002	4003	5	0		100.00	20.00	T1	120.00	N	-
18	SI	30/09/2010	CAM004	4002	6	0		45.00	9.00	T1	54.00	N	-
19	SI	30/09/2010	HAS004	4000	7	0		12.00	2.40	T1	14.40	N	-
							Totals:	4,951.60	179.70		5,131.30		

Shows a list of all invoices produced including the Net, VAT and Gross Amounts

Customer Activity – Detailed (Report CSTACTD.report)

Date:	27/06/2012	Page: 1
Time:	12:20:36	

Total Photo Limited
Customer Activity (Detailed)

Date From:	01/01/1980	Customer From:	
Date To:	30/09/2010	Customer To:	ZZZZZZZZ
Transaction From:	1	N/C From:	
Transaction To:	99,999,999	N/C To:	99999999
Inc b/fwd transaction:	No	Dept From:	0
Exc later payment:	No	Dept To:	999

** NOTE: All report values are shown in Base Currency, unless otherwise indicated **

A/C: CAM004 **Name:** Campbell & Dunn **Contact:** **Tel:**

No	Type	Date	Ref	N/C	Details	Dept	T/C	Value	O/S	Debit	Credit	V	B
11	SI	30/09/2010		9998	Opening Balance	0	T9	2,056.85 *	2,056.85	2,056.85		-	-
18	SI	30/09/2010	6	4002		0	T1	54.00 *	54.00	54.00		N	-
					Totals:			2,110.85	2,110.85	2,110.85			

Amount Outstanding	2,110.85
Amount Paid this period	0.00
Credit Limit £	2,500.00
Turnover YTD	2,101.85

A/C: HAS004 **Name:** Mr W Haslam **Contact:** **Tel:**

No	Type	Date	Ref	N/C	Details	Dept	T/C	Value	O/S	Debit	Credit	V	B
7	SI	30/09/2010		9998	Opening Balance	0	T9	309.85 *	309.85	309.85		-	-
14	SI	30/09/2010	2	4000		0	T1	29.40 *	29.40	29.40		N	-
19	SI	30/09/2010	7	4000		0	T1	14.40 *	14.40	14.40		N	-
					Totals:			353.65	353.65	353.65			

Amount Outstanding	353.65
Amount Paid this period	0.00
Credit Limit £	500.00
Turnover YTD	346.35

A/C: LUL002 **Name:** Lullabies Nursery **Contact:** **Tel:**

No	Type	Date	Ref	N/C	Details	Dept	T/C	Value	O/S	Debit	Credit	V	B
12	SI	30/09/2010		9998	Opening Balance	0	T9	726.90		726.90		-	-
17	SI	30/09/2010	5	4003		0	T1	120.00 *	120.00	120.00		N	-
92	SR	30/09/2010		1200	Sales Receipt	0	T9	726.90			726.90	-	N
					Totals:			120.00	120.00	846.90	726.90		

Amount Outstanding	120.00
Amount Paid this period	726.90
Credit Limit £	1,500.00
Turnover YTD	826.90

A/C: PAR006 **Name:** Miss S Pargenter **Contact:** **Tel:**

No	Type	Date	Ref	N/C	Details	Dept	T/C	Value	O/S	Debit	Credit	V	B
9	SI	30/09/2010		9998	Opening Balance	0	T9	650.00 *	650.00	650.00		-	-
15	SI	30/09/2010	3	4000		0	T1	14.40 *	14.40	14.40		N	-
84	SC	30/09/2010	1	4000	Returned faulty	0	T1	14.40 *	-14.40		14.40	N	-
					Totals:			650.00	650.00	664.40	14.40		

Amount Outstanding	650.00
Amount Paid this period	0.00
Credit Limit £	1,000.00
Turnover YTD	650.00

| Date: | 27/06/2012 | Total Photo Limited | Page: | 2 |
| Time: | 12:20:36 | Customer Activity (Detailed) | | |

A/C: PAS002 Name: Mrs T Pashby   Contact: Tel:

No	Type	Date	Ref	N/C	Details	Dept	T/C	Value	O/S	Debit	Credit	V	B
10	SI	30/09/2010		9998	Opening Balance	0	T9	89.50		89.50		.	.
110	SC	30/09/2010	BADDBT	8100	Bad Debt Write Off	0	T9	89.50			89.50	.	.
					Totals:			0.00	0.00	89.50	89.50		

Amount Outstanding   0.00
Amount Paid this period   0.00
Credit Limit £   500.00
Turnover YTD   89.50

A/C: POP002 Name: Mrs H Poppy   Contact: Tel:

No	Type	Date	Ref	N/C	Details	Dept	T/C	Value	O/S	Debit	Credit	V	B
8	SI	30/09/2010		9998	Opening Balance	0	T9	220.00 p	100.00	220.00		.	.
13	SI	30/09/2010	1	4000		0	T1	126.00 *	126.00	126.00		N	.
93	SR	30/09/2010		1225	Sales Receipt	0	T9	120.00			120.00	.	N
					Totals:			226.00	226.00	346.00	120.00		

Amount Outstanding   226.00
Amount Paid this period   120.00
Credit Limit £   500.00
Turnover YTD   325.00

A/C: SMI009 Name: Mr A Smith   Contact: Tel:

No	Type	Date	Ref	N/C	Details	Dept	T/C	Value	O/S	Debit	Credit	V	B
16	SI	30/09/2010	4	4001		0	T1	720.00 *	720.00	720.00		N	.
					Totals:			720.00	720.00	720.00			

Amount Outstanding   720.00
Amount Paid this period   0.00
Credit Limit £   1,000.00
Turnover YTD   600.00

Shows all transactions for customers (e.g. purchases and receipts)

Customer Address List (Report)

| Date: | 19/10/2009 | TotalPhoto Ltd | Page: | 1 |
| Time: | 20:51:56 | Customer Address List | | |

Customer From:
Customer To: ZZZZZZZ

A/C	Name & Address	Contact Name	Telephone	Fax
CAM004	Campbell & Dunn 12 The Beeches Miltonby Lancashire LN87 9PP			
HAS004	W Haslam 22 Brown Street Miltonby Lancashire LN87 6FD			
LUL002	Lullabies Nursery 104 Victoria Road Miltonby Lancashire LN87 5PS			
PAR006	S Pargenter 11 Alexandra Park Miltonby Lancashire LN87 2WD			

Shows address details, contact name etc for customers

3 Supplier reports

Aged Creditors Analysis (Report SPLAGED.report)

Date:	29/06/2012		**Total Photo Limited**		Page:	1
Time:	11:39:18		**Aged Creditors Analysis (Detailed)**			

Date From:	01/01/1980	Supplier From:	
Date To:	29/06/2012	Supplier To:	ZZZZZZZZ

Include future transactions: No
Exclude later payments: No

** NOTE: All report values are shown in Base Currency, unless otherwise indicated **

A/C:	AP004	Name:	Arthur's Photographic Equipment Ltd	Contact:	Jennie Reeves	Tel:	0121 299 0192

No:	Type	Date	Ref	Details	Balance	Future	Current	Period 1	Period 2	Period 3	Older
6	PI	30/09/2010	O/Bal	Opening Balance	11,275.00	0.00	0.00	0.00	0.00	0.00	11,275.00
79	PC	30/09/2010	134C	Returned cameras	-2,531.99	0.00	0.00	0.00	0.00	0.00	-2,531.99
				Totals:	8,743.01	0.00	0.00	0.00	0.00	0.00	8,743.01

Turnover: 9,165.01
Credit Limit £ 20,000.00

A/C:	MF001	Name:	Mackay Films Ltd	Contact:	Carl Richardson	Tel:	01828 827493

No:	Type	Date	Ref	Details	Balance	Future	Current	Period 1	Period 2	Period 3	Older
1	PI	30/09/2010	O/Bal	Opening Balance	345.36	0.00	0.00	0.00	0.00	0.00	345.36
74	PI	30/09/2010	1341		250.51	0.00	0.00	0.00	0.00	0.00	250.51
				Totals:	595.87	0.00	0.00	0.00	0.00	0.00	595.87

Turnover: 554.12
Credit Limit £ 2,500.00

A/C:	MP002	Name:	Mills Paper Products	Contact:	Mr Shaun Squire	Tel:	01726 378918

No:	Type	Date	Ref	Details	Balance	Future	Current	Period 1	Period 2	Period 3	Older
4	PI	30/09/2010	O/Bal	Opening Balance	4,920.30	0.00	0.00	0.00	0.00	0.00	4,920.30
78	PI	30/09/2010			195.02	0.00	0.00	0.00	0.00	0.00	195.02
				Totals:	5,115.32	0.00	0.00	0.00	0.00	0.00	5,115.32

Turnover: 5,082.82
Credit Limit £ 8,000.00

A/C:	OI001	Name:	Octopus Inks Ltd	Contact:	Sheila Cribbley	Tel:	0191 252 4132

No:	Type	Date	Ref	Details	Balance	Future	Current	Period 1	Period 2	Period 3	Older
5	PI	30/09/2010	O/Bal	Opening Balance	550.20	0.00	0.00	0.00	0.00	0.00	550.20
77	PI	30/09/2010	2203		371.14	0.00	0.00	0.00	0.00	0.00	371.14
				Totals:	921.34	0.00	0.00	0.00	0.00	0.00	921.34

Turnover: 859.48
Credit Limit £ 2,500.00

A/C:	SC003	Name:	The Stationery Cupboard	Contact:	Alan Pensill	Tel:	01482 417378

No:	Type	Date	Ref	Details	Balance	Future	Current	Period 1	Period 2	Period 3	Older
75	PI	30/09/2010	209		17.58	0.00	0.00	0.00	0.00	0.00	17.58
76	PI	30/09/2010	216		94.70	0.00	0.00	0.00	0.00	0.00	94.70
				Totals:	112.28	0.00	0.00	0.00	0.00	0.00	112.28

Turnover: 468.57
Credit Limit £ 1,000.00

				Grand Totals:	15,487.82	0.00	0.00	0.00	0.00	0.00	15,487.82

Shows the outstanding creditor balances and the how long the debts have been in existence

Supplier Activity Report (Report SPALCTD.report)

Date:	29/06/2012				**Total Photo Limited**				Page:	1
Time:	11:43:25				**Supplier Activity (Detailed)**					

Date From:	01/01/1980			Supplier From:			
Date To:	29/06/2012			Supplier To:	ZZZZZZZZ		
Transaction From:	1			N/C From:			
Transaction To:	99,999,999			N/C To:	99999999		
Inc b/fwd transaction:	No			Dept From:	0		
Exc later payment:	No			Dept To:	999		

** NOTE: All report values are shown in Base Currency, unless otherwise indicated **

A/C: AP004   Name: Arthur's Photographic Equipment Ltd   Contact: Jennie Reeves   Tel: 0121 299 0192

No	Type	Date	Ref	N/C	Details	Dept	T/C	Value	O/S	Debit	Credit	V	B
6	PI	30/09/2010	O/Bal	9998	Opening Balance	0	T9	11,275.00 *	11,275.00		11,275.00	-	-
79	PC	30/09/2010	134C	0022	Returned cameras	0	T1	2,531.99 *	-2,531.99	2,531.99		N	-
					Totals:			8,743.01	8,743.01	2,531.99	11,275.00		

Amount Outstanding	8,743.01
Amount paid this period	0.00
Credit Limit £	20,000.00
Turnover YTD	9,165.01

A/C: KF001   Name: K2 Films Ltd   Contact: Kim Nakajima   Tel: 0207 867 6599

No	Type	Date	Ref	N/C	Details	Dept	T/C	Value	O/S	Debit	Credit	V	B
2	PI	30/09/2010	O/Bal	9998	Opening Balance	0	T9	1,726.55	0.00		1,726.55	-	-
84	PP	30/09/2010	00246	1200	Purchase Payment	0	T9	1,726.55	0.00	1,726.55		-	N
					Totals:			0.00	0.00	1,726.55	1,726.55		

Amount Outstanding	0.00
Amount paid this period	1,726.55
Credit Limit £	5,000.00
Turnover YTD	1,726.55

A/C: MF001   Name: Mackay Films Ltd   Contact: Carl Richardson   Tel: 01828 827493

No	Type	Date	Ref	N/C	Details	Dept	T/C	Value	O/S	Debit	Credit	V	B
1	PI	30/09/2010	O/Bal	9998	Opening Balance	0	T9	345.36 *	345.36		345.36	-	-
74	PI	30/09/2010	1341	5000		0	T1	250.51 *	250.51		250.51	N	-
					Totals:			595.87	595.87	0.00	595.87		

Amount Outstanding	595.87
Amount paid this period	0.00
Credit Limit £	2,500.00
Turnover YTD	554.12

A/C: MP002   Name: Mills Paper Products   Contact: Mr Shaun Squire   Tel: 01726 378918

No	Type	Date	Ref	N/C	Details	Dept	T/C	Value	O/S	Debit	Credit	V	B
4	PI	30/09/2010	O/Bal	9998	Opening Balance	0	T9	4,920.30 *	4,920.30		4,920.30	-	-
78	PI	30/09/2010		5001		0	T1	195.02 *	195.02		195.02	N	-
					Totals:			5,115.32	5,115.32	0.00	5,115.32		

Amount Outstanding	5,115.32
Amount paid this period	0.00
Credit Limit £	8,000.00
Turnover YTD	5,082.82

A/C: OI001   Name: Octopus Inks Ltd   Contact: Sheila Cribbley   Tel: 0191 252 4132

No	Type	Date	Ref	N/C	Details	Dept	T/C	Value	O/S	Debit	Credit	V	B
5	PI	30/09/2010	O/Bal	9998	Opening Balance	0	T9	550.20 *	550.20		550.20	-	-
77	PI	30/09/2010	2203	5002		0	T1	371.14 *	371.14		371.14	N	-
					Totals:			921.34	921.34	0.00	921.34		

Amount Outstanding	921.34
Amount paid this period	0.00
Credit Limit £	2,500.00
Turnover YTD	859.48

| Date: | 29/06/2012 | | | **Total Photo Limited** | | | | Page: | 2 | |
| Time: | 11:43:25 | | | **Supplier Activity (Detailed)** | | | | | | |

| A/C: | SC003 | Name: | The Stationery Cupboard | | Contact: | Alan Pensill | | Tel: | 01482 417378 | |

No	Type	Date	Ref	N/C	Details	Dept	T/C	Value	O/S	Debit	Credit	V	B
3	PI	30/09/2010	O/Bal	9998	Opening Balance	0	T9	375.00	0.00		375.00	-	-
75	PI	30/09/2010	209	5003		0	T1	17.58 *	17.58		17.58	N	-
76	PI	30/09/2010	216	5003		0	T1	94.70 *	94.70		94.70	N	-
83	PP	30/09/2010	00245	1200	Purchase Payment	0	T9	375.00	0.00	375.00		-	N
					Totals:			112.28	112.28	375.00	487.28		

Amount Outstanding	112.28
Amount paid this period	375.00
Credit Limit £	1,000.00
Turnover YTD	468.57

Shows all transactions for a single, or range of, suppliers, including purchases, returns, payments etc

Day Book Supplier Invoices (Report SPLDYIVD.report)

| Date: | 29/06/2012 | | **Total Photo Limited** | | Page: | 1 |
| Time: | 11:44:12 | | **Day Books: Supplier Invoices (Detailed)** | | | |

Date From:	01/01/1980		Supplier From:	
Date To:	31/12/2019		Supplier To:	ZZZZZZZZ
Transaction From:	1		N/C From:	
Transaction To:	99,999,999		N/C To:	99999999
Dept From:	0			
Dept To:	999			

Tran No.	Type	Date	A/C Ref	N/C	Inv Ref	Dept	Details	Net Amount	Tax Amount	T/C	Gross Amount	V	B
1	PI	30/09/2010	MF001	9998	O/Bal	0	Opening Balance	345.36	0.00	T9	345.36	-	-
2	PI	30/09/2010	KF001	9998	O/Bal	0	Opening Balance	1,726.55	0.00	T9	1,726.55	-	-
3	PI	30/09/2010	SC003	9998	O/Bal	0	Opening Balance	375.00	0.00	T9	375.00	-	-
4	PI	30/09/2010	MP002	9998	O/Bal	0	Opening Balance	4,920.30	0.00	T9	4,920.30	-	-
5	PI	30/09/2010	OI001	9998	O/Bal	0	Opening Balance	550.20	0.00	T9	550.20	-	-
6	PI	30/09/2010	AP004	9998	O/Bal	0	Opening Balance	11,275.00	0.00	T9	11,275.00	-	-
74	PI	30/09/2010	MF001	5000	1341	0		208.76	41.75	T1	250.51	N	-
75	PI	30/09/2010	SC003	5003	209	0		14.65	2.93	T1	17.58	N	-
76	PI	30/09/2010	SC003	5003	216	0		78.92	15.78	T1	94.70	N	-
77	PI	30/09/2010	OI001	5002	2203	0		309.28	61.86	T1	371.14	N	-
78	PI	30/09/2010	MP002	5001		0		162.52	32.50	T1	195.02	N	-
							Totals	19,966.54	154.82		20,121.36		

Shows the list of all invoices received.

Supplier Details List (Report SPLADDL.report)

Date:	19/10/2009		TotalPhoto Ltd			Page:	1
Time:	20:58:33		Supplier Address List				

Supplier From:
Supplier To: ZZZZZZZ

A/C	Name	Contact	Telephone	Fax
AF004	Arthur's Photographic Equipment Ltd 77 Overton Lane Birmingham BM97 8YK	Jennie Reeves	0121 299 0192	
KF001	K2 Films Ltd Tokyo House 72-84 Great Milne Street London WC4 6DD	Kim Nakajima	0207 867 6599	
MF001	Mackay Films Ltd 33 West Parade Miltonby Lancashire LN87 7HD	Carl Richardson	01828 827493	
MP002	Mills Paper Products 405 Ream Road Bradford West Yorkshire	Mr Shaun Squire	01726 378918	

Shows a list of suppliers with contact details

4 Bank reports

Day Books: Bank Payments (Report BNKBPD.report)

Date:	29/06/2012		Total Photo Limited			Page:	1
Time:	11:45:23		Day Books: Bank Payments (Detailed)				

Date From:	01/01/1980				Bank From:	1200
Date To:	31/12/2019				Bank To:	1200

Transaction From:	1			N/C From:	
Transaction To:	99,999,999			N/C To:	99999999

Dept From:	0
Dept To:	999

Bank: 1200   Currency: Pound Sterling

No	Type	N/C	Date	Ref	Details	Dept	Net £	Tax £	T/C	Gross £	V	B	Bank Rec. Date
80	BP	7502	30/09/2010		Arrow Phone	0	107.65	21.53	T1	129.18	N	N	
81	BP	6201	30/09/2010		Cricket Handbook	0	55.00	0.00	T9	55.00	-	R	05/10/2010
82	BP	7304	30/09/2010		Parking Permit	0	45.00	0.00	T9	45.00	-	N	
91	BP	6201	30/09/2010	DD/STO	North West Radio	0	200.00	40.00	T1	240.00	N	R	05/10/2010
92	BP	6201	30/10/2010	DD/STO	North West Radio	0	200.00	40.00	T1	240.00	N	N	
93	BP	6201	30/11/2010	DD/STO	North West Radio	0	200.00	40.00	T1	240.00	N	N	
94	BP	6201	30/12/2010	DD/STO	North West Radio	0	200.00	40.00	T1	240.00	N	N	
106	BP	7901	30/09/2010			0	31.41	0.00	T9	31.41	-	R	05/10/2010
					Totals £		1,039.06	181.53		1,220.59			

Shows all payments from the chosen bank account

Day Books: Bank Receipts (Report BNKBRD.report)

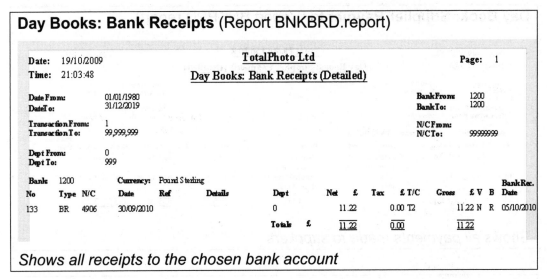

Date:	19/10/2009			**TotalPhoto Ltd**					Page:	1	
Time:	21:03:48			**Day Books: Bank Receipts (Detailed)**							

Date From:	01/01/1980			BankFrom:	1200	
DateTo:	31/12/2019			BankTo:	1200	
Transaction From:	1			N/CFrom:		
TransactionTo:	99,999,999			N/CTo:	99999999	
Dept From:	0					
DeptTo:	999					

Bank: 1200   Currency: Pound Sterling

No	Type	N/C	Date	Ref	Details	Dept	Net £	Tax	£ T/C	Gross £ V B	BankRec. Date
133	BR	4906	30/09/2010			0	11.22	0.00	T2	11.22 N R	05/10/2010
						Totals £	11.22	0.00		11.22	

Shows all receipts to the chosen bank account

Similar reports are available for cash, and credit card, payments and receipts

Reconciled Transactions (Report BANKREC.report)

Date:	29/06/2012		**Total Photo Limited**		Page:	1
Time:	11:50:44		**Bank Reconciled Transactions**			

Bank Reconciled On: 30/09/2010

No	Type	Date	A/C	N/C	Dept	Ref	Details	Net	Tax	T/C
29	JD	30/09/2010	1200	1200	0	O/Bal	Opening Balance	10,293.00	0.00	T9

Bank Reconciled On: 05/10/2010

No	Type	Date	A/C	N/C	Dept	Ref	Details	Net	Tax	T/C
81	BP	30/09/2010	1200	6201	0		Cricket Handbook	55.00	0.00	T9
90	JD	30/09/2010	1200	1200	0	TRANS	Bank Transfer	150.00	0.00	T9
91	BP	30/09/2010	1200	6201	0	DD/STO	North West Radio	200.00	40.00	T1
103	JC	30/09/2010	1200	1200	0	Journal	Correction of error	30.00	0.00	T9
106	BP	30/09/2010	1200	7901	0			31.41	0.00	T9
107	BR	30/09/2010	1200	4906	0			11.22	0.00	T9

Shows all bank transactions that have been successfully matched and reconciled to the bank statement

Day Book: Supplier Payments (Report BNKPPD.report)

Date:	16/07/2012				**Total Photo Limited**				Page:	1
Time:	11:37:36				**Day Books: Supplier Payments (Detailed)**					

Date From:	01/01/1980			Bank From:	1200
DateTo:	31/12/2019			Bank To:	1200

Transaction From:	1			Supplier From:	
Transaction To:	99,999,999			Supplier To:	ZZZZZZZZ

Bank   1200   Currency   Pound Sterling

No	Type	A/C	Date	Ref	Details	Net £	Tax	£ T/C	Gross £	V B	Bank Rec. Date
83	PP	SC003	30/09/2010	00245	Purchase Payment	375.00	0.00	T9	375.00	- N	
		-	30/09/2010	O/Bal	375.00 to PI 3						
84	PP	KF001	30/09/2010	00246	Purchase Payment	1,726.55	0.00	T9	1,726.55	- N	
		-	30/09/2010	O/Bal	1726.55 to PI 2						
					Totals £	2,101.55	0.00		2,101.55		

Shows all payments made to suppliers

Day Book: Customer Receipts (Report BNKSRD.report)

Date:	29/06/2012				**Total Photo Limited**				Page:	1
Time:	12:23:15				**Day Books: Customer Receipts (Detailed)**					

Date From:	01/01/1980			Bank From:	1200
DateTo:	31/12/2019			Bank To:	1200

Transaction From:	1			Customer From:	
Transaction To:	99,999,999			Customer To:	ZZZZZZZZ

Bank   1200   Currency   Pound Sterling

No	Type	A/C	Date	Ref	Details	Net £	Tax	£ T/C	Gross £	V B	Bank Rec. Date
87	SR	LUL002	30/09/2010		Sales Receipt	726.90	0.00	T9	726.90	- N	
		-	30/09/2010	O/Bal	726.90 to SI 12						
88	SR	POP002	30/09/2010		Sales Receipt	120.00	0.00	T9	120.00	- N	
		-	30/09/2010	O/Bal	120.00 to SI 8						
					Totals £	846.90	0.00		846.90		

Shows all receipts from customers

Unreconciled Payments Report (Report BNKUPAY.report)

Date:	16/07/2012			**Total Photo Limited**			Page:	1
Time:	11:42:11			**Unreconciled Payments**				

Date From:	01/01/1980			Bank From:	1200
DateTo:	31/12/2019			Bank To:	1200

Transaction From:	1
Transaction To:	99,999,999

Bank   1200   Bank Account Name   Bank Current Account   Currency   Pound Sterling

No	Type	Date	Ref	Details	Amount £
80	BP	30/09/2010		Arrow Phone	129.18
82	BP	30/09/2010		Parking Permit	45.00
83	PP	30/09/2010	00245	Purchase Payment	375.00
84	PP	30/09/2010	00246	Purchase Payment	1,726.55
92	BP	30/10/2010	DD/STO	North West Radio	240.00
93	BP	30/11/2010	DD/STO	North West Radio	240.00
94	BP	30/12/2010	DD/STO	North West Radio	240.00
101	JC	30/09/2010	TRANS	Bank Transfer	23.24
				Total £	3,018.97

Shows all payments which have not been matched and reconciled against a bank statement

Unreconciled Receipts Report (Report BNKURCT.report)

Date:	29/06/2012		**Total Photo Limited**				Page:	1
Time:	12:26:32		**Unreconciled Receipts**					

Date From:	01/01/1980			Bank From:	1200
Date To:	31/12/2019			Bank To:	1200

Transaction From:	1
Transaction To:	99,999,999

Bank	1200		Bank Account Name	Bank Current Account		Currency	Pound Sterling		
No	Type	Date	Ref	Details				Amount	£
87	SR	30/09/2010		Sales Receipt					726.90
88	SR	30/09/2010		Sales Receipt					120.00
							Total £		846.90

Shows all receipts which have not been matched and reconciled against a bank statement

5 Other reports

Nominal List (Report NOMLIST.report)

Date:	19/10/2009		**TotalPhoto Ltd**	Page:	1
Time:	21:33:11		**Nominal List**		

N/C From:	
N/C To:	99999999

N/C	Name
0010	Freehold Property
0011	Leasehold Property
0020	Plant and Machinery
0021	Plant/Machinery Depreciation
0022	Photographic Equipment
0023	Depreciation (Photo Eqpmt)
0030	Office Equipment
0031	Office Equipment Depreciation
0040	Furniture and Fixtures
0041	Furniture/Fixture Depreciation
0050	Motor Vehicles
0051	Motor Vehicles Depreciation
1001	Stock
1002	Work in Progress
1003	Finished Goods
1100	Debtors Control Account
1101	Sundry Debtors
1102	Other Debtors
1103	Prepayments
1200	Bank Current Account

Shows all heading codes within the chat of accounts

Amending company details and managing data

12

KNOWLEDGE

2.2 Review transaction process and identify any errors

2.3 Respond appropriately to any transaction errors and problems

3.4 Import and export data and link to other systems and software

CONTENTS

1 Amending data

2 Exporting data

1 Amending data

As we have already seen, one of the most common ways to correct an error is by means of a journal. This is essentially a book-keeping solution, using a double entry to correct or amend an earlier error. Sometimes, however, it is necessary to change a transaction we have entered that we cannot correct with a journal.

For example, in the TotalPhoto Case Study we entered a credit note for returned cameras. We cannot enter a journal to correct this as Sage does not allow us to post a journal to a control account (the Creditors Control Account). If we needed to correct this we must go through file maintenance this can be found in File task bar menu:

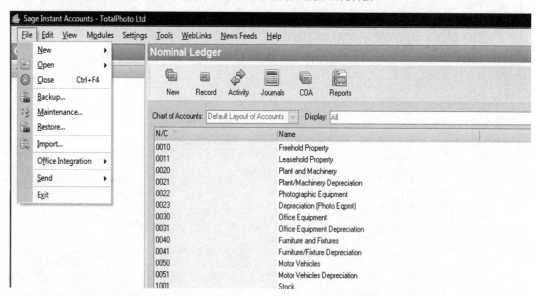

Within file maintenance we have the choice of searching for the item we are trying to correct by many different criteria. One good way to do this is to use the account reference.

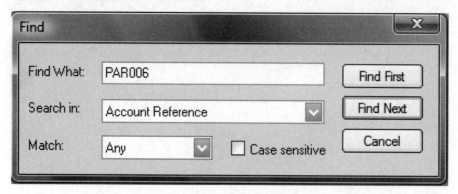

By searching by the account reference of the transaction we are trying to find we can search through the transactions until we find the one we want by clicking [Find Next]

Once we have found the transaction we want we have the choice of either deleting or amending the transaction by clicking the buttons at the top of the screen.

Pressing delete brings up the following screen:

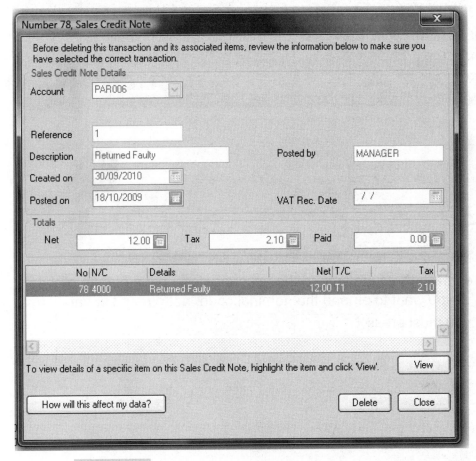

Clicking [Delete] will delete the transaction from the ledger although the fact that it existed will always be shown and it will be offset by a deleting entry as opposed to being completely removed from the ledgers.

Pressing edit brings up the following screen:

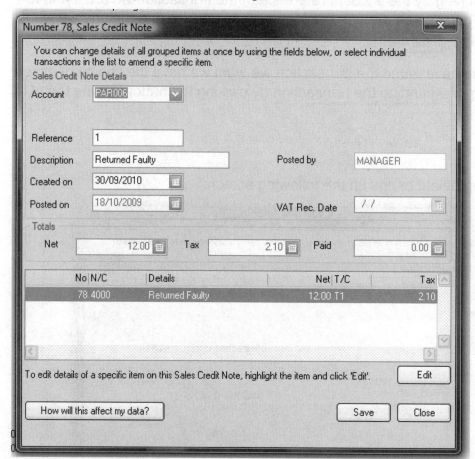

This screen allows you to amend the account, description or date of the invoice. If you want to amend the nominal code, net amount or vat amount you must press [Edit].

This brings up this screen:

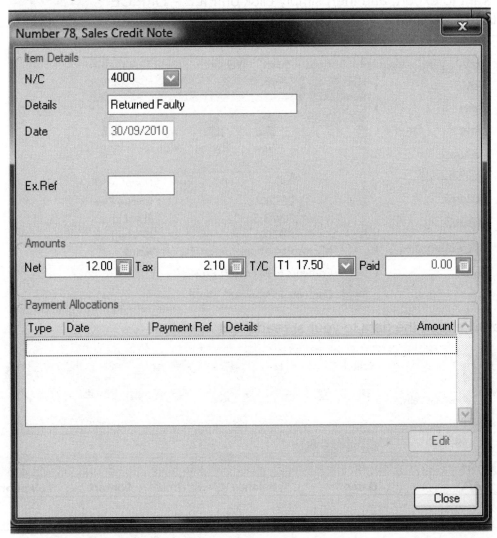

This allows you to amend the nominal code, details, net amount, VAT amount and tax code.

2 Exporting data

You may wish to export data from SAGE to another program – for example, a spreadsheet.

Let us imagine that you want to export details of the company's credit suppliers to Microsoft Excel.

Bring up the supplier list screen as required, highlight whichever records you want to export, and then simply click on FILE – OFFICE INTEGRATION – CONTENTS TO MICROSOFT EXCEL (or whichever program you want to export to).

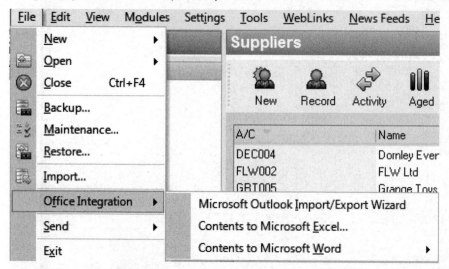

This will export the data to your spreadsheet as below:

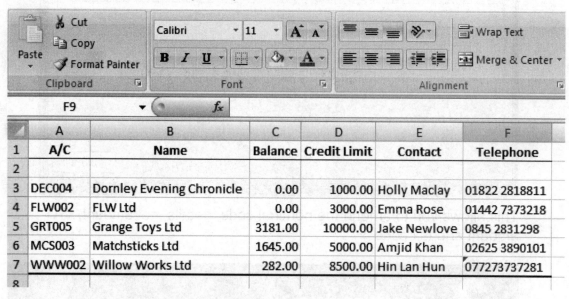

	A	B	C	D	E	F
1	A/C	Name	Balance	Credit Limit	Contact	Telephone
2						
3	DEC004	Dornley Evening Chronicle	0.00	1000.00	Holly Maclay	01822 2818811
4	FLW002	FLW Ltd	0.00	3000.00	Emma Rose	01442 7373218
5	GRT005	Grange Toys Ltd	3181.00	10000.00	Jake Newlove	0845 2831298
6	MCS003	Matchsticks Ltd	1645.00	5000.00	Amjid Khan	02625 3890101
7	WWW002	Willow Works Ltd	282.00	8500.00	Hin Lan Hun	077273737281
8						

WORKBOOK

QUESTIONS

QUESTIONS

Practice assessment questions

Part one

This assessment comprises short written tasks which should be undertaken in supervised assessment conditions in one session of no more than 45 minutes duration.

Task 1.1

From the following list of accounting documents, match the most appropriate one to each of the descriptions:

A   Sales Invoice

B   Credit Note

C   Purchase Order

D   Debit Note

E   Customer Statement

F   Supplier Statement

1   A request to a supplier requesting a credit note following a delivery of faulty or otherwise unwanted goods.

2   A document issued by a customer formally requesting the order of goods or services.

3   A report issued to a customer (usually monthly), showing a list of all transactions and monies received, and all outstanding balances.

4   A request for payment issued by the seller of goods or services to the buyer.

5   A report received by an organisation (usually on a monthly basis) from its suppliers which lists all transactions, monies paid, and outstanding balances.

6   A document which reverses all or part of an invoice relating to damaged or otherwise returned goods.

Task 1.2

(a) Explain why "Jones" may not be a good code to use for one of our customers' accounts – even though she is called Alice Jones.

....

....

....

....

(b) Give an example of a code which would be more appropriate for Alice Jones's account.

....

Task 1.3

It is late on Friday afternoon, and you are on sick leave from work. Your manager, Angela, rings you at home to say that there is a crisis in the office – she needs access to a client's file that you have been working on. This is a matter of some urgency. She asks you for your password, so that she can access the file, print it out, and then work on it over the weekend.

What should you do? Explain your answer.

....

....

....

....

....

....

....

....

....

....

....

....

....

....

....

Task 1.4

You receive the following email at work.

To:	Accountingtechnician@webnet.com
From:	Friend@bali.net
Date:	30 September 2010 03:27:24
Att:	Virusblocker.exe

Hi

Please be aware that there is a new virus which has been spreading in the past 24 hours. If your computer becomes infected the virus will wipe your hard drive completely, leaving the computer worthless and losing all your data.

The virus is called "Happydays"; if you receive any emails with this name you should delete them.

It is possible to block this virus; all you need to do is open the attached file ("Virusblocker.exe") and follow the instructions on screen.

Happy computing!

Explain what you should do on receiving this e-mail.

....

....

....

....

....

....

....

....

....

....

....

....

....

....

Task 1.5

Any computer which is connected to the 'outside world' is potentially at risk of infection from a virus.

(a) Identify **two** different ways in which a virus could be introduced to a computer.

....

....

....

....

....

(b) Identify **two** policies or procedures that an organisation could introduce to minimise the risk of infection from a computer virus.

....

....

....

....

....

(c) Identify **two** possible effects that a virus could have on a computer system.

....

....

....

....

....

Task 1.6

Your colleague, Hassan, has borrowed a company laptop to work on some files whilst he travels by train to a conference. Identify <u>two</u> possible threats to data security that could occur as a result of him doing this.

....

....

....

....

....

....

KAPLAN PUBLISHING

Task 1.7

The Data Protection Act (1998) places particular emphasis on the importance of safeguarding "sensitive data". Which of the following would be considered "sensitive data", under the terms of the Act?

An individual's date of birth and address	
A company's VAT registration number	
An individual's preferred brand of chocolate	
An individual's religious views	
An individual's membership of a Trade Union	

Task 1.8

Data can be exported from a computerised accountancy program to another package, and vice versa. Which type of package is most likely to be used in conjunction with data from the accounting system for each of the following uses:

Representation of monthly sales figures in the form of a graph	
Sending a letter to all suppliers informing them of a change of website details	

Part two

This assessment comprises an assignment that can be completed in four separate sessions. The time allowed to complete the assignment is 5 hours and a suggested time allowance for each section is 75 minutes.

Instructions to candidate

This assignment is based on an existing business, Justin Timbercrafts, an organisation that makes small wooden toys which it sells to independent toy stores and the public. The owner of the business is Justin Wilson, who operates as a sole trader.

At the start of business Justin operated a manual book-keeping system, but has now decided that from 1st August 19XX the accounting system will become computerised. You are employed as an accounting technician in the business.

You can assume that all documentation within this assessment has been checked for accuracy and duly authorised by Justin.

Sales are to be analysed in four ways:

- The Jungle Collection
- The Farm Collection
- The Pets Collection
- Cash Sales – to members of the public at the small factory shop

The business is registered for VAT, and the rate charged on all items is the basic rate of 20.0%

All expenditure should be analysed as you feel appropriate.

You should set the system date at 31st August 20XX – the financial year starts in July 20XX.

You should ensure that your name and the date appear on all print outs.

Session One

Task 1.1

(a) Refer to the customer details below and set up customer records to open Sales Ledger Accounts for each customer.

Customer Details

Customer Name, Address and Contact Details	Customer Account Code	Customer Account Details
Toyways plc 88 Main Street Longstan LG18 5DF Tel: 01872 62819203 Contact: Brian Mason	TW003	Credit Limit = £5,000 Payment Terms = 28 days Opening Balance = £1,235.76 (relates to invoice00288 dated 15th July 20XX)
Perfect Pastimes Ltd Hubley Industrial Estate Hubley HB29 7FD Tel: 07719 3612819 Contact: Stan Hartley	PP002	Credit Limit = £15,000 Payment Terms = 28 days Opening Balance = £13,209.34 (relates to invoice 00291 dated 17th July 20XX)
Happykidz Ltd Churchill Shopping Centre Fearnley FN88 3DS Tel: 0727 4792982 Contact: Shane Humphries	HK006	Credit Limit = £8,000 Payment Terms = 28 days Opening Balance = £342.98 (relates to invoice 00299 dated 28th July 20XX)
Prettypops Ltd 10 St Bart's Row Ganningly GN33 2WQ Tel: 0845 19828282 Contact: Betty Chamberlain	PP004	Credit Limit = £5,000 Payment Terms = 28 days Opening Balance = £190.87 (relates to invoice 00212 dated 17th July 20XX)

(b) Save your work and print a Customer List.

Task 1.2

Refer to the Supplier Details below and create supplier records to open Purchase Ledger Accounts for each supplier.

Supplier name, address and contact details	Supplier Account Code	Supplier Account Details
Matchsticks Ltd Unit 66 Haxton HC99 7TG Tel : 02625 3890101 Contact: Amjid Khan	MCS003	Credit Limit = £5000 Payment Terms = 30 days Opening Balance = £1943.26 (relates to Invoice 2033 dated 18 July 20XX)
Willow Works Ltd Ceder House Lanchester LN33 7DK Tel: 07727 3737281 Contact: Hin Lan Hun	WWW002	Credit Limit = £8,500 Payment Terms= 30 days Opening Balance = £288.29 (relates to Invoice 38842 dated 20 July 20XX)
Grange Toys Ltd The Lodge Kilminster KG18 6GC Tel : 0845 2831298 Contact: Jake Newlove	GRT005	Credit Limit = £10,000 Payment Terms = 30 days Opening Balance = £4,277.50 (relates to Invoice GT2640 dated 12 July 20XX)
FLW Ltd 199 Duncan Avenue Hurtleby HB28 4FS Tel : 07227 2903832 Contact: Emma Rose	FLW002	Credit Limit = £3,000 Payment Terms = 14 days Opening Balance = £923.46 (relates to Invoice 2727 dated 20 July 20XX)
Dornley Evening Chronicle 11 Dundee Street Dornley DN22 6FD Tel : 01822 2818811 Contact: Holly Maclay	DEC004	Credit Limit = £1,000 Payment Terms = 30 days Opening Balance = £0.00

(c)   Save your work and print a Supplier List.

Task 1.3

Enter the following opening balances into the appropriate nominal accounts, making any amendments you feel are necessary.

Account Name	£	£
Motor Vehicles	4,586.00	
Office Equipment	1,354.00	
Equipment and Tools	2,330.00	
Bank	1,203.30	
Petty Cash	150.00	
Sales Ledger Control Account*	14978.95	
Purchase Ledger Control Account*		7432.51
Sales – Jungle Collection		17,293.50
Sales – Farm Collection		19,224.70
Sales – Pets Collection		10,260.45
Cash Sales		5,431.40
Capital		10,000.00
Rent and Rates	2,400.00	
Insurance	720.00	
Advertising	1,420.00	
Purchases of materials	28,344.80	
Office stationery	2,350.00	
Miscellaneous Motor Expenses	9805.51	
	69,642.56	**69,642.56**

Task 1.4

(a)   Use the appropriate software tool to check for data errors

(b)   Print a screen shot of the data verification screen

(c)   Make any necessary corrections

Task 1.5

(a) Print a trial balance

(b) Check the accuracy of the trial balance and, if necessary, correct any errors

Task 1.6 – Ignore this task if you are continuing to Session 2 without a break

(a) Back up your work to a suitable storage media. Your assessor will tell you what storage media you should use

(b) Print a screen shot of the backup screen showing the location of back up data

Session Two

Task 2.1

You have received the following e-mail from FLW Ltd (a supplier).

To:	accounts@justintimbercrafts.co.uk
From:	emmarose@networks.com
Date:	29/07/20XX

Hi there

Just to let you know that we are moving! From 31st July our new address will be Emsley House, Radleigh, RD77 3ED.

Our new phone number is 01442 7373218

Please ensure that you update all records with this change in address

Kind regards

Emma

(a) Print a screen shot of the supplier's record with the current address and telephone number.

(b) Enter the new address and telephone number into the accounting system.

(c) Print a screen shot of the supplier's details with the amended address and telephone number.

Task 2.2

Refer to the following sales invoices and credit note:

Justin Timbercrafts
27 West Lane
Dornley
DN22 4RD
"Quality Wooden Toys at Affordable Prices"

INVOICE 00300
Tax Point : 2nd August 20XX   VAT Registration Number: 4839101298

Happykidz Ltd
Churchill Shopping Centre
Fearnley
FN88 3DS

Farm Collections × 8	£7.00	£56.00
Jungle Collections × 10	£9.00	£90.00
		£146.00
VAT @ 20.0%		£29.20
TOTAL FOR PAYMENT		£175.20

Terms: 30 days

Justin Timbercrafts
27 West Lane
Dornley
DN22 4RD
"Quality Wooden Toys at Affordable Prices"

INVOICE 00301
Tax Point : 2nd August 20XX   VAT Registration Number: 4839101298

Toyways plc
88 Main Street
Longstan
LG18 5DF

Farm Collections × 5	£7.00	£35.00
Jungle Collections × 5	£9.00	£45.00
Pets Collections × 5	£9.00	£45.00
		£125.00
VAT @ 20.0%		£25.00
TOTAL FOR PAYMENT		£150.00

Terms: 30 days

Justin Timbercrafts
27 West Lane
Dornley
DN22 4RD
"Quality Wooden Toys at Affordable Prices"

INVOICE 00302
Tax Point : 4th August 20XX   VAT Registration Number: 4839101298

Happykidz Ltd
Churchill Shopping Centre
Fearnley
FN88 3DS

Farm Collections × 4	£7.00	£28.00
Pets Collections × 8	£9.00	£72.00
		£100.00
VAT @ 20.0%		£20.00
TOTAL FOR PAYMENT		£120.00

Terms: 30 days

Justin Timbercrafts
27 West Lane
Dornley
DN22 4RD
"Quality Wooden Toys at Affordable Prices"

CREDIT NOTE 55
Tax Point : 2nd August 20XX   VAT Registration Number: 4839101298

Happykidz Ltd
Churchill Shopping Centre
Fearnley
FN88 3DS

Farm Collections × 2 (Broken)	£7.00	£14.00
VAT @ 20.0%		£2.80
TOTAL FOR PAYMENT		£16.80

Terms: 30 days

(a) Enter the sales invoices and credit notes into the computerised accounting system.

Refer to the following summary of purchase invoices:

Date	Supplier	Invoice No	Gross £	VAT £	Net £	Materials	Advertising
2/8/XX	Dornley Evening Chronicle	2929/11	156.00	26.00	130.00		130.00
3/8/XX	Grange Toys Ltd	GT2882	1,272.00	212.00	1,060.00	1,060.00	
6/8/XX	Willow Works Ltd	99128	288.00	48.00	240.00	240.00	
	Totals		**1,716.00**	**286.00**	**1,430.00**	**1,300.00**	**130.00**

(b) Enter the purchase invoices into the computerised accounting system.

Refer to the following summary of payments received from customers and made to suppliers:

Cheque / BACS Receipts Listing

Date	Details	Customer	£	How Received
03 Aug XX	Payment of opening	Toyways plc	1235.76	Cheque
05 Aug XX	balance	Happykidz Ltd	342.98	BACS
	Payment of opening balance			

Cheques Paid Listing

Date	Details	Supplier	£	Cheque Number
04 Aug XX	Payment of opening	FLW Ltd	923.46	0012671
04 Aug XX	balance	Matchsticks Ltd	1943.26	0012672
	Payment of opening balance			

(c) Enter the receipts and payments into the computer, making sure you allocate all amounts as shown in the details column.

Refer to the following email from Justin:

email
From : Justin@justintimbercrafts.co.uk
To : accounts@justintimbercrafts.co.uk
Date: 5 August 20XX
Subject: Prettypops Ltd
Hi I'm afraid that Prettypops Ltd have gone into liquidation – I've just had a letter from their administrators. It looks most unlikely we will get anything for their outstanding account – which stands at £190.87. Please write this amount off as a bad debt. Thanks Justin

(d) Print a customer statement for Prettypops Ltd, showing the balance of £190.87. Then make the entries into the computer to write off the amount of £190.87 owing from Prettypops Ltd. Ignore VAT. Print a new customer statement showing the amount written off and the new balance of nil.

Task 2.3

Refer to the following petty cash vouchers:

Petty Cash Voucher	
Date 3 August 20XX Ref: PC 54	
Details	
Window cleaner (*zero rated for VAT purposes*) Receipt attached	£20.00

Petty Cash Voucher	
Date 5 August 20XX	
Ref: PC 55	
Details	
5 × New calculators	£20.00
VAT	£4.00
Total	£24.00
Receipt attached	

Enter the petty cash payments into the computer.

Task 2.4

Refer to the following receipts issued for cash sales in the factory shop:

Receipt	**Receipt**
No: 1326	No: 1327
2nd August 20XX	4th August 20XX
Received by cheque for toys (A Smith)	Received by cheque for toys (R Wilkins)
£78.24 including VAT	£102.30 including VAT

(a)   Enter these receipts in the computer.

Refer to the following email from Justin:

email
From : Justin@justintimbercrafts.co.uk
To : accounts@justintimbercrafts.co.uk
Date: 4 August 20XX
Subject: Drawings
Hi I've withdrawn £200 from the bank as a donation to my favourite charity – cheque number 0012673. Thanks Justin

(b)   Enter this transaction in the computer.

Task 2.5

Refer to the following email from Justin:

email
From : Justin@justintimbercrafts.co.uk
To : accounts@justintimbercrafts.co.uk
Date: 5 August 20XX
Subject: Opening Balances
Hi I've just realised that the list of opening balances I gave you for entry to the new computer system contained an error. The balance of £1,420.00 for advertising actually contains a sum of £120.00 which should be classified as Insurance – sorry, my mistake! Could you please correct this for me? Thanks Justin

Enter the appropriate journal into the computer to correct the error in the opening balances.

Task 2.6

(a) Use the appropriate software tool to check for data errors

(b) Print a screen shot of the data verification screen

(c) Make any necessary corrections

Task 2.7

(a) Print a trial balance as at 14 August 20XX

(b) Check the accuracy of the trial balance and, if necessary, correct any errors

Task 2.8

Ignore this task if you are continuing to Session 3 without a break

(a) Back up your work to a suitable storage media. Your assessor will tell you what storage media you should use.

(b) Print a screen shot of the backup screen showing the location of back up data.

Session Three

Refer to the following email from Justin:

---

email

From : Justin@justintimbercrafts.co.uk

To : accounts@justintimbercrafts.co.uk

Date: 6 August 20XX

Subject: Opening Balances

Hi

Could you please enter the details of a new customer that I have agreed terms with this morning?

The details are:

Funnystuff Ltd

31 Yew Tree Way

Hedgefield

HD43 2WA

The settlement terms are 14 days with a credit limit of £1,000.

Please select an appropriate Customer Account Code for this customer

Thanks

Justin

Task 3.1

(a) Set up a new customer record for Funnystuff Ltd to open a sales ledger account with an opening balance of nil.

(b) Print a screen shot of the new customer's record card showing the name and address details.

Refer to the following sales invoices:

Justin Timbercrafts
27 West Lane
Dornley
DN22 4RD
"Quality Wooden Toys at Affordable Prices"

INVOICE 00303
Tax Point : 6th August 20XX
VAT Registration Number: 4839101298

Funnystuff Ltd
31 Yew Tree Way
Hedgefield
HD43 2WA

Farm Collections × 5	£7.00	£35.00
Pets Collections × 5	£9.00	£45.00
		£80.00
VAT @ 20.0%		£16.00
TOTAL FOR PAYMENT		£96.00

Terms: 14 days

Justin Timbercrafts
27 West Lane
Dornley
DN22 4RD
"Quality Wooden Toys at Affordable Prices"

INVOICE 00304
Tax Point : 6th August 20XX
VAT Registration Number: 4839101298

Toyways plc
88 Main Street
Longstan
LG18 5DF

Pets Collections × 30	£9.00	£270.00
		£270.00
VAT @ 20.0%		£54.00
TOTAL FOR PAYMENT		£324.00

Terms: 28 days

Task 3.2

(a)   Enter the sales invoices into the computer.

Refer to the following summary of purchases invoices:

Date	Supplier Name	Invoice Number	Gross £	VAT £	Net £	Materials £	Advertising £
8/8/XX	Matchsticks Ltd	3178	1680.00	280.00	1400.00	1400.00	
10/8/XX	Grange Toys Ltd	GT2916	672.00	112.00	560.00	560.00	
		Total	**2352.00**	**392.00**	**1960.00**	**1960.00**	

(b)   Enter the purchase invoices into the computer.

Refer to the following summary of payments received from and made to suppliers:

Cheque / BACS Receipts Listing

Date	Details	Customer	£	How Received
11/8/XX	Payment of Invoice 00300 including credit note CN55	Happykidz Ltd	158.40	BACS

Cheques Paid Listing

Date	Details	Supplier	£	Cheque Number
11/8/XX 14/8/XX	Payment of opening balance	Willow Works Ltd	288.29	0012674
14/8/XX	Part-payment of opening balance	Grange Toys Ltd	3000.00	0012675
	Payment of Invoice 2929/11	Dornley Evening Chronicle	156.00	0012676

(c)   Enter the receipts and payments into the computer, making sure you allocate all amounts as shown in the details column.

Refer to the following petty cash vouchers:

Petty Cash Voucher

Date 12 August 20XX

Ref: PC 56

Details	
Train fare – exempt for VAT	£14.80
Receipt attached	

Petty Cash Voucher

Date 14 August 20XX
Ref: PC 57

Details	
Photocopy paper	£8.50
VAT	£1.70
Total	£10.20
Receipt attached	

Task 3.3

Enter the petty cash payments into the computer.

Refer to the following e-mail from Justin:

---

email

From : Justin@justintimbercrafts.co.uk

To : accounts@justintimbercrafts.co.uk

Date: 14 August 20XX

Subject: Grant

Hi

I don't know if you remember me telling you but I applied for a grant a few months ago – and guess what! We've just got a cheque through from the grant agency for £240 – I've taken it to the bank this morning when I was passing.

Could you enter it into the system please?

Thanks

Justin

Task 3.4

(a)   Enter this grant income into the computer.

Refer to the following receipt for the purchase of a new picture, paid for by petty cash. Use voucher code PC57 for this transaction:

Receipt Number 1289

Art of the Matter

Kitchener Shopping Centre

Miltonby

VAT Reg: 343 4839 47

Date : 14 August 20XX

Received from Justin Timbercrafts, by cash, for original print

£25 inc VAT

(b)   Enter the details of this transaction into the computer. This is a picture for the office wall, so should be coded to "Office Stationery"

Refer to the following schedule of standing orders:

Date	Payee	Expense	£
18/10	P Smith	Rent	400.00
18/10	Dornley Borough Council	Rates	120.00

Assume both of these are zero-rated.

(c)   Enter the standing orders into the computer as a bank payment, and post them as necessary to ensure that August's transactions are entered into the computer.

Refer to the post-it note left on your desk by Justin shown below:

Hi

Sorry – the grant was only for £220, not £240 as I said.

Justin

Task 3.5

Enter the following journal to correct the error:

Journal – 20 August 20XX	Dr £	Cr £
Bank		20.00
Miscellaneous Income	20.00	
Being correction of error recording amount of grant income received		

Task 3.6

(a) Use the appropriate software tool to check for data errors

(b) Print a screen shot of the data verification screen

(c) Make any necessary corrections

Task 3.7

(a) Print a trial balance as at 31 August 20XX

(b) Check the accuracy of the trial balance and, if necessary, correct any errors

Task 3.8

Ignore this task if you are continuing to Session 4 without a break

(a) Back up your work to a suitable storage media. Your assessor will tell you what storage media you should use

(b) Print a screen shot of the backup screen showing the location of back up data

Session Four

Refer to the email below from Justin:

email
From : Justin@justintimbercrafts.co.uk
To : accounts@justintimbercrafts.co.uk
Date: 31st August 20XX
Subject: Petty cash
Hi Please transfer £94.00 from the bank account to the petty cash account to reimburse the petty cash float – this should reinstate it to £150.00 Thanks Justin

Task 4.1

(a)   Enter this transaction into the computer.

(b)   Print the petty cash account.

Refer to the following bank statement:

MIDWEST BANK plc
109 Church Street
Dornley
DN12 5DE

Justin Timbercrafts
27 West Lane
Dornley
DN22 4RD

Account Number : 341723810

31 August 20XX

Statement of Account – Sheet 819

Date (20XX)	Details	Paid out £	Paid in £	Balance £
1 August	Opening Balance			1203.30 Cr
05/08/20XX	BGC		1235.76	2439.06 Cr
05/08/20XX	BACS Receipt		342.98	2782.04 Cr
10/08/20XX	Chq 0012671	923.46		1858.58 Cr
12/08/20XX	Chq 0012672	1943.26		84.68 Dr
12/08/20XX	Chq 0012673	200.00		284.68 Dr
15/08/20XX	BGC		220.00	64.68 Dr
15/08/20XX	Chq 0012675	3000.00		3064.68 Dr
15/08/20XX	Direct Debit	400.00		3464.68 Dr
16/08/20XX	Direct Debit	120.00		3584.68 Dr
28/08/20XX	Bank Charges	32.00		3616.68 Dr
31/08/20XX	Closing Balance			3616.68 Dr

CR = Credit
DR = Debit

Task 4.2

(a) Enter the bank charges (no VAT) which have not yet been accounted for

(b) Reconcile the bank statement. If the bank statement does not reconcile check your work and make the necessary corrections

Task 4.3

(a) Back up your work to a suitable storage media. Your assessor will tell you what storage media you should use

(b) Print a screen shot of the backup screen showing the location of back up data

Task 4.4

Print the following reports

- The sales day book (customer invoices)
- The sales returns day book (customer credits)
- The purchases day book (supplier invoices)
- All sales ledger accounts
- All purchase ledger accounts

Task 4.5

(a) Generate an Aged Creditor Analysis showing all outstanding items and print a copy

(b) Generate an Aged Debtors Analysis showing all outstanding items and print a copy

(c) Export the Aged Debtors Analysis to a spreadsheet and print a copy of the spreadsheet. You do not need to make any alterations to the spreadsheet

Task 4.6

Print Statements of Account for Happykidz Ltd and Perfect Pastimes Ltd.

Task 4.7

Print an overdue account letter for Perfect Pastimes Ltd.

Task 4.8

Print all journal entries.

Task 4.9

(a)   Print an audit trail

(b)   Print a Trial Balance as at 31 August 20XX

Task 4.10

Use the relevant software tool to clear month end turnover totals and print a screen shot of the on screen instruction to clear month end turnover totals.

ANSWERS

Practice assessment answers

Part one

This assessment comprises short written tasks which should be undertaken in supervised assessment conditions in one session of no more than 45 minutes duration.

Task 1.1

From the following list of accounting documents, match the most appropriate one to each of the descriptions:

A   Sales Invoice

B   Credit Note

C   Purchase Order

D   Debit Note

E   Customer Statement

F   Supplier Statement

1   A request to a supplier requesting a credit note following a delivery of faulty or otherwise unwanted goods   *D – Debit Note*

2   A document issued by a customer formally requesting the order of goods or services   *C – Purchase Order*

3   A report issued to a customer (usually monthly), showing a list of all transactions and monies received, and all outstanding balances   *E – Customer Statement*

4   A request for payment issued by the seller of goods or services to the buyer   *A – Sales Invoice*

5   A report received by an organisation (usually on a monthly basis) from its suppliers which lists all transactions, monies paid, and outstanding balances   *F – Supplier Statement*

6   A document which reverses all or part of an invoice relating to damaged or otherwise returned goods   *B – Credit Note*

Task 1.2

(a) Explain why "Jones" may not be a good code to use for one of our customers' accounts – even though she is called Alice Jones.

Because the organisation is likely to have more than one customer called 'Jones', each one will need a unique identifying code. 'Jones' does not identify this customer from another one with the same name.

(b) Give an example of a code which would be more appropriate for Alice Jones's account.

The organisation should consider using an Alphanumeric code – e.g. 'JONESA001'

Task 1.3

It is late on Friday afternoon, and you are on sick leave from work. Your colleague, Angela, rings you at home to say that there is a crisis in the office – she needs access to a client's file that you have been working on. This is a matter of some urgency. She asks you for your password, so that she can access the file, print it out, and then work on it over the weekend.

What should you do? Explain your answer.

You should firstly make absolutely sure that it really is your colleague that you are speaking to on the phone – if you have any doubts at all you should ring her back on the office number. Having assured yourself of this, you should then ask to speak to your manager to confirm the authenticity of the request. You should NOT divulge your password to your colleague. You could ask your manager if there is no other way that the file can be accessed- e.g. by an IT technician. If there is no other way, you should provide your manager with your password, as this is a reasonable request from your supervisor. On your return to work on Monday morning you should immediately change your password to minimise the risk of unauthorised access to your system.

Task 1.4

You receive the following e-mail at work.

To: Accountingtechnician@webnet.com

From: Friend@bali.net

Date: 30 September 2010   03:27:24

Att: Virusblocker.exe

Hi

Please be aware that there is a new virus which has been spreading in the past 24 hours. If your computer becomes infected the virus will wipe your hard drive completely, leaving the computer worthless and losing all your data.

The virus is called "Happydays"; if you receive any emails with this name you should delete them.

It is possible to block this virus; all you need to do is open the attached file ("Virusblocker.exe") and follow the instructions on screen.

Happy computing!

Explain what you should do on receiving this e-mail.

You should report the e-mail to your supervisor and/or IT Manager. Under no circumstances should you open the attached file – if this is a malicious e-mail the attachment is likely to contain a virus which could infect your machine, others on the network, and other e-mails in your address book.

Task 1.5

Any computer which is connected to the 'outside world' is potentially at risk of infection from a virus.

(a)   Identify **two** different ways in which a virus could be introduced to a computer.

Via an e-mail attachment

Via a website

Via an infected memory stick or disk

Via an infected piece of software

(b)   Identify **two** policies or procedures that an organisation could introduce to minimise the risk of infection from a computer virus.

Installation of firewalls

Installation of virus tracking software

Policies regarding internet and e-mail use by employees

(c)   Identify **two** possible effects that a virus could have on a computer system.

Amendment or deletion of files

Wiping of hard drive

Slowing computer down

Infecting other computers that are inter-connected

Reading passwords or sharing other sensitive data

Task 1.6

Your colleague, Hassan, has borrowed a company laptop to work on some files whilst he travels by train to a conference. Identify <u>two</u> possible threats to data security that could occur as a result of him doing this.

A fellow passenger could read confidential information, either in hard copy or on the screen, whilst he is working on it.

The laptop or memory stick containing data could be accidentally left on the train or at the conference.

Task 1.7

The Data Protection Act (1998) places particular emphasis on the importance of safeguarding "sensitive data". Which of the following would be considered "sensitive data", under the terms of the Act?

An individual's date of birth and address	**Yes**
A company's VAT registration number	**No**
An individual's preferred brand of chocolate	**No**
An individual's religious views	**Yes**
An individual's membership of a Trade Union	**Yes**

Task 1.8

Data can be exported from a computerised accountancy program to another package, and vice versa. Which type of package is most likely to be used in conjunction with data from the accounting system for each of the following uses:

Representation of monthly sales figures in the form of a graph	*A spreadsheet (e.g. Microsoft Excel)*
Sending a letter to all suppliers informing them of a change of website details	*A word processor (e.g. Microsoft Word)*

Part two

Note: *the exact printout you produce may not exactly match the suggested answer. Nevertheless, the information contained in your answers should be broadly the same.*

Session One

Task 1.1

Justin Timbercrafts
Customer Address List

Customer From:
Customer To: ZZZZZZZ

A/C	Name & Address	Contact Name	Telephone
HKD06	Happykidz Ltd Churchill Shopping Centre Fearnley FN88 3DS	Shane Humphries	0727 4792982
PP002	Perfect Pastimes Ltd Hubley Industrial Estate Hubley HB29 7FD	Stan Hartley	07719 3612819
PP004	Prettypops Ltd 10 St Bart's Row Ganringly GN33 2WQ	Betty Chamberlain	0845 19828282
TW003	Toyways plc 88 Main Street Longstan LG18 5DF	Brian Mason	01872 62819203

Task 1.2

Justin Timbercrafts

Supplier Address List

Supplier From:
Supplier To: ZZZZZZZ

A/C	Name	Contact	Telephone
DEC004	Domley Evening Chronicle 11 Dundee Street Domley DN22 6FD	Holly Maclay	01822 2818811
FLW002	FLW Ltd 199 Duncan Avenue Hurtleby HB28 4FS	Emma Rose	01442 7373218
GRT005	Grange Toys Ltd The Lodge Kilminster KG18 6GC	Jake Newlove	0845 2831298
MCS003	Matchsticks Ltd Unit 66 Haxton HC99 7TG	Amjid Khan	02625 3890101
WWW002	Willow Works Ltd Ceder House Lanchester LN33 7DK	Hin Lan Hun	07727373728

Task 1.3   Answer shown in later task.

Task 1.4   Answer will depend on errors by students.

Task 1.5

Date: 25/08/2010
Time: 21:18:20
Page: 1

Justin Timbercrafts
Period Trial Balance

To Period: Month 12, July 2011

N/C	Name	Debit	Credit
0020	Equipment and Tools	2,330.00	
0030	Office Equipment	1,354.00	
0050	Motor Vehicles	4,586.00	
1100	Debtors Control Account	14,978.95	
1200	Bank Current Account	1,203.30	
1230	Petty Cash	150.00	
2100	Creditors Control Account		7,432.51
3000	Capital		10,000.00
4000	Sales Jungle Collection		17,293.50
4001	Sales Farm Collection		19,224.70
4002	Sales Pets Collection		10,260.45
4003	Cash Sales		5,431.40
5000	Materials Purchased	28,344.80	
6201	Advertising	1,420.00	
7100	Rent & Rates	2,400.00	
7304	Miscellaneous Motor Expenses	9,805.51	
7504	Office Stationery	2,350.00	
8204	Insurance	720.00	
	Totals:	69,642.56	69,642.56

Task 1.6 Answer will depend on back up used by student.

Session Two

Task 2.1 (a)

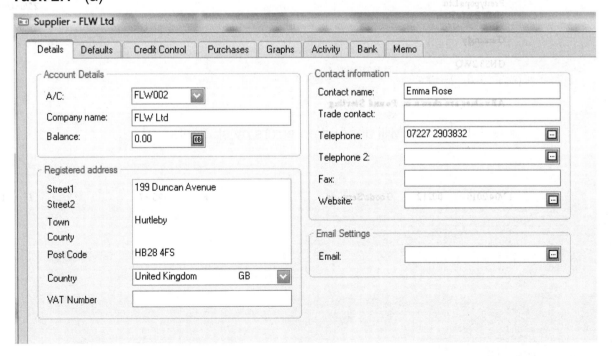

(c)

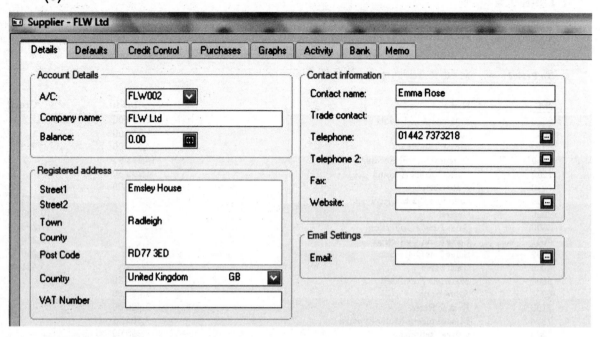

Task 2.2

(a)   Answer in later task.

(b)   Answer in later task.

(c)   Answer in later task.

(d)

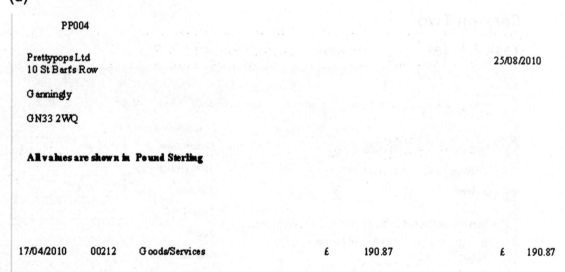

KAPLAN PUBLISHING

Justin Timbercrafts
27 West Lane
Dornley

PP004

Prettypops Ltd
10 St Bart's Row

25/08/2010

Garningly

GN33 2WQ

All values are shown in Pound Sterling

| 17/04/2010 | 00212 | Goods/Services | £ | 190.87 | | | £ | 190.87 |
| 05/08/2010 | | Credit | | | £ | 190.87 | £ | 0.00 |

Task 2.3

Answer in later task.

Task 2.4

Answer in later task.

Task 2.5

Answer in later task.

Task 2.6

Answer will depend on errors by student.

Task 2.7

Date: 29/06/2012
Time: 13:31:05

Justin Timbercrafts
Period Trial Balance

Page: 1

To Period: Month 12, June 2011

N/C	Name	Debit	Credit
0020	Equipment and Tools	2,330.00	
0030	Office Equipment	1,354.00	
0050	Motor Vehicles	4,586.00	
1100	Debtors Control Account	13,637.74	
1200	Bank Current Account		104.14
1230	Petty Cash	106.00	
2100	Creditors Control Account		6,281.79
2200	Sales Tax Control Account		101.49
2201	Purchase Tax Control Account	290.00	
3000	Capital		10,000.00
4000	Sales - Jungle Collection		17,428.50
4001	Sales - Farm Collection		19,329.70
4002	Sales - Pets Collection		10,377.45
4003	Cash Sales		5,581.85
5000	Materials Purchased	29,644.80	
6201	Advertising	1,430.00	
7100	Rent and Rates	2,400.00	
7304	Miscellaneous Motor Expenses	9,805.51	
7504	Office Stationery	2,370.00	
7801	Cleaning	20.00	
8100	Bad Debt Write Off	190.87	
8200	Donations	200.00	
8204	Insurance	840.00	
	Totals:	69,204.92	69,204.92

Task 2.8

Answers will depend on choices made by student.

Session Three

Task 3.1

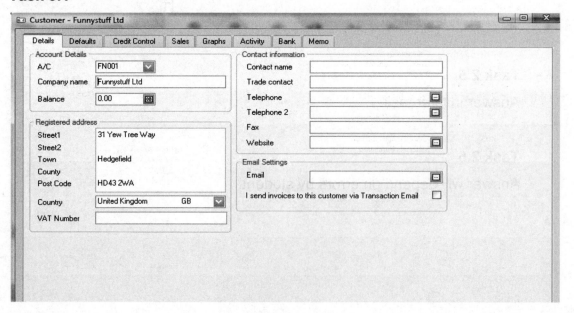

Task 3.2

Answer in later task.

Task 3.3

Answer in later task.

Task 3.4

Answer in later task.

Task 3.5

Answer in later task.

Task 3.6

Answer will depend on student errors.

Task 3.7

Date:	29/06/2012		**Justin Timbercrafts**		Page:	1
Time:	13:56:40		**Period Trial Balance**			

To Period: Month 12, June 2011

N/C	Name	Debit	Credit
0020	Equipment and Tools	2,330.00	
0030	Office Equipment	1,354.00	
0050	Motor Vehicles	4,586.00	
1100	Debtors Control Account	13,899.34	
1200	Bank Current Account		3,690.03
1230	Petty Cash	56.00	
2100	Creditors Control Account		5,189.50
2200	Sales Tax Control Account		171.49
2201	Purchase Tax Control Account	687.87	
3000	Capital		10,000.00
4000	Sales - Jungle Collection		17,428.50
4001	Sales - Farm Collection		19,364.70
4002	Sales - Pets Collection		10,692.45
4003	Cash Sales		5,581.85
4900	Miscellaneous Income		220.00
5000	Materials Purchased	31,604.80	
6201	Advertising	1,430.00	
7100	Rent and Rates	2,920.00	
7304	Miscellaneous Motor Expenses	9,805.51	
7400	Travelling	14.80	
7504	Office Stationery	2,399.33	
7801	Cleaning	20.00	
8100	Bad Debt Write Off	190.87	
8200	Donations	200.00	
8204	Insurance	840.00	
	Totals:	72,338.52	72,338.52

Task 3.8

Answers will depend on choices made by student.

Session Four

Task 4.1

Task 4.2

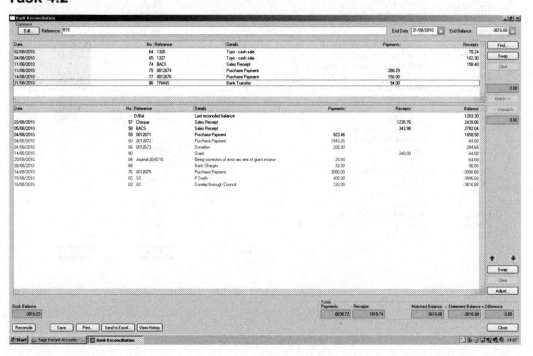

Task 4.3

Answer will depend on student choices.

Task 4.4

Sales Day Book

Date:	02/07/2012					**Justin Timbercrafts**				Page:	1	
Time:	10:32:28					**Day Books: Customer Invoices (Detailed)**						

Date From:	01/01/1980					Customer From:	
Date To:	31/12/2019					Customer To:	ZZZZZZZZ
Transaction From:	1					N/C From:	
Transaction To:	99,999,999					N/C To:	99999999
Dept From:	0						
Dept To:	999						

Tran No.	Type	Date	A/C Ref	N/C	Inv Ref	Dept.	Details	Net Amount	Tax Amount	T/C	Gross Amount	V	B
1	SI	15/07/2010	TW003	9998	O/Bal inv	0	Opening Balance	1,235.76	0.00	T9	1,235.76	-	-
2	SI	17/07/2010	PP002	9998	O/Bal inv	0	Opening Balance	13,209.34	0.00	T9	13,209.34	-	-
3	SI	28/07/2010	HK006	9998	O/Bal inv	0	Opening Balance	342.98	0.00	T9	342.98	-	-
4	SI	17/07/2010	PP004	9998	O/Bal inv	0	Opening Balance	190.87	0.00	T9	190.87	-	-
41	SI	02/08/2010	HK006	4001	00300	0	Farm Collections x 8	56.00	11.20	T1	67.20	N	-
42	SI	02/08/2010	HK006	4000	00300	0	Jungle Collections x 10	90.00	18.00	T1	108.00	N	-
43	SI	02/08/2010	TW003	4001	00301	0	Farm Collections x 5	35.00	7.00	T1	42.00	N	-
44	SI	02/08/2010	TW003	4000	00301	0	Jungle Collections x 5	45.00	9.00	T1	54.00	N	-
45	SI	02/08/2010	TW003	4002	00301	0	Pets Collections x 5	45.00	9.00	T1	54.00	N	-
46	SI	04/08/2010	HK006	4001	00302	0	Farm collections x 4	28.00	5.60	T1	33.60	N	-
47	SI	04/08/2010	HK006	4002	00302	0	Pets collections x 8	72.00	14.40	T1	86.40	N	-
69	SI	06/08/2010	FN001	4001	00303	0	Farm collections x 5	35.00	7.00	T1	42.00	N	-
70	SI	06/08/2010	FN001	4002	00303	0	Pets collections x 5	45.00	9.00	T1	54.00	N	-
71	SI	06/08/2010	TW003	4002	00304	0	Pets collections x 30	270.00	54.00	T1	324.00	N	-
							Totals:	15,699.95	144.20		15,844.15		

Sales Returns Day Book

Date:	02/07/2012					**Justin Timbercrafts**				Page:	1	
Time:	10:33:21					**Day Books: Customer Credits (Detailed)**						

Date From:	01/01/1980					Customer From:	
Date To:	31/12/2019					Customer To:	ZZZZZZZZ
Transaction From:	1					N/C From:	
Transaction To:	99,999,999					N/C To:	99999999
Dept From:	0						
Dept To:	999						

Tran No.	Type	Date	A/C Ref	N/C	Inv Ref	Dept.	Details	Net Amount	Tax Amount	T/C	Gross Amount	V	B
48	SC	02/08/2010	HK006	4001	55	0	Farm Collections x 2 (Broken)	14.00	2.80	T1	16.80	N	-
61	SC	05/08/2010	PP004	8100	BADDBT	0	Bad Debt Write Off	190.87	0.00	T9	190.87	-	-
							Totals:	204.87	2.80		207.67		

Purchases Day Book

Date:	02/07/2012			**Justin Timbercrafts**						Page:	1	
Time:	10:35:32			**Day Books: Supplier Invoices (Detailed)**								

Date From:	01/01/1980		Supplier From:	
Date To:	31/12/2019		Supplier To:	ZZZZZZZZ
Transaction From:	1		N/C From:	
Transaction To:	99,999,999		N/C To:	99999999
Dept From:	0			
Dept To:	999			

Tran No.	Type	Date	A/C Ref	N/C	Inv Ref	Dept	Details	Net Amount	Tax Amount	T/C	Gross Amount	V	B
5	PI	18/07/2010	MCS003	9998	O/Bal inv	0	Opening Balance	1,943.26	0.00	T9	1,943.26	-	-
6	PI	20/07/2010	WWW002	9998	O/Bal inv	0	Opening Balance	288.29	0.00	T9	288.29	-	-
7	PI	12/07/2010	GRT005	9998	O/Bal inv	0	Opening Balance	4,277.50	0.00	T9	4,277.50	-	-
8	PI	20/07/2010	FLW002	9998	O/Bal inv	0	Opening Balance	923.46	0.00	T9	923.46	-	-
54	PI	02/08/2010	DEC004	6201	2929/11	0	Advertising	130.00	26.00	T1	156.00	N	-
55	PI	03/08/2010	GRT005	5000	GT2882	0	Materials	1,060.00	212.00	T1	1,272.00	N	-
56	PI	06/08/2010	WWW002	5000	99128	0	Materials	240.00	48.00	T1	288.00	N	-
72	PI	08/08/2010	MCS003	5000	3178	0	Materials	1,400.00	280.00	T1	1,680.00	N	-
73	PI	10/08/2010	GRT005	5000	GT2916	0	Materials	560.00	112.00	T1	672.00	N	-
							Totals	10,822.51	678.00		11,500.51		

Sales Ledger Accounts

Date:	02/07/2012			**Justin Timbercrafts**			Page:	1
Time:	10:37:03			**Supplier Activity (Summary)**				

Date From:	01/01/1980		Supplier From:	
Date To:	02/07/2012		Supplier To:	ZZZZZZZZ
Inc b/fwd transaction:	No		Transaction From:	1
Exc later payment:	No		Transaction To:	99,999,999

** NOTE: All report values are shown in Base Currency, unless otherwise indicated **

A/C:	DEC004	Name:	Domley Evening Chronicle	Contact:	Holly Maclay	Tel:	01822 2818811

No	Items	Type	Date	Ref	Details	Value	O/S	Debit	Credit
54	1	PI	02/08/2010	2929/11	Advertising	156.00			156.00
77	1	PP	14/08/2010	0012676	Purchase Payment	156.00	0.00	156.00	
					Totals:	0.00	0.00	156.00	156.00

Amount Outstanding:	0.00	
Amount paid this period	156.00	
Credit Limit £	1,000.00	

A/C:	FLW002	Name:	FLW Ltd	Contact:	Emma Rose	Tel:	01442 7373218

No	Items	Type	Date	Ref	Details	Value	O/S	Debit	Credit
8	1	PI	20/07/2010	O/Bal inv	Opening Balance	923.46	0.00		923.46
59	1	PP	04/08/2010	0012671	Purchase Payment	923.46	0.00	923.46	
					Totals:	0.00	0.00	923.46	923.46

Amount Outstanding:	0.00	
Amount paid this period	923.46	
Credit Limit £	3,000.00	

A/C:	GRT005	Name:	Grange Toys Ltd	Contact:	Jake Newlove	Tel:	0845 2831298

No	Items	Type	Date	Ref	Details	Value	O/S	Debit	Credit
7	1	PI	12/07/2010	O/Bal inv	Opening Balance	4,277.50p	1,277.50		4,277.50
55	1	PI	03/08/2010	GT2882	Materials	1,272.00*	1,272.00		1,272.00
73	1	PI	10/08/2010	GT2916	Materials	672.00*	672.00		672.00
76	1	PP	14/08/2010	0012675	Purchase Payment	3,000.00	0.00	3,000.00	
					Totals:	3,221.50	3,221.50	3,000.00	6,221.50

Amount Outstanding:	3,221.50	
Amount paid this period	3,000.00	
Credit Limit £	10,000.00	

A/C:	MCS003	Name:	Matchsticks Ltd	Contact:	Amjid Khan	Tel:	02625 3890101

No	Items	Type	Date	Ref	Details	Value	O/S	Debit	Credit
5	1	PI	18/07/2010	O/Bal inv	Opening Balance	1,943.26	0.00		1,943.26
60	1	PP	04/08/2010	0012672	Purchase Payment	1,943.26	0.00	1,943.26	
72	1	PI	08/08/2010	3178	Materials	1,680.00*	1,680.00		1,680.00
					Totals:	1,680.00	1,680.00	1,943.26	3,623.26

Amount Outstanding:	1,680.00	
Amount paid this period	1,943.26	
Credit Limit £	5,000.00	

Date: 02/07/2012
Time: 10:37:03

Justin Timbercrafts
Supplier Activity (Summary)

Page: 2

A/C: WWW002 **Name:** Willow Works Ltd **Contact:** Hin Lan Hun **Tel:** 07727 3737281

No	Items	Type	Date	Ref	Details	Value	O/S	Debit	Credit
6	1	PI	20/07/2010	O/Bal inv	Opening Balance	288.29	0.00		288.29
56	1	PI	06/08/2010	99128	Materials	288.00*	288.00		288.00
75	1	PP	11/08/2010	0012674	Purchase Payment	288.29	0.00	288.29	
					Totals:	288.00	288.00	288.29	576.29

Amount Outstanding: 288.00
Amount paid this period 288.29
Credit Limit £ 8,500.00

Purchase Ledger Accounts

Date: 02/07/2012
Time: 10:37:51

Justin Timbercrafts
Customer Activity (Summary)

Page: 1

Date From:	01/01/1980	Customer From:	
Date To:	02/07/2012	Customer To:	ZZZZZZZZ
Inc b/fwd transaction:	No	Transaction From:	1
Exc later payment:	No	Transaction To:	99,999,999

** NOTE: All report values are shown in Base Currency, unless otherwise indicated **

A/C: FN001 **Name:** Funnystuff Ltd **Contact:** **Tel:**

No	Items	Type	Date	Ref	Details	Value	O/S	Debit	Credit
69	2	SI	06/08/2010	00303	Farm collections x 5	96.00 *	96.00	96.00	
						96.00	96.00	96.00	0.00

Amount Outstanding 96.00
Amount Paid this period 0.00
Credit Limit £ 1,000.00

A/C: HK006 **Name:** Happykidz Ltd **Contact:** Shane Humphries **Tel:** 0727 4792982

No	Items	Type	Date	Ref	Details	Value	O/S	Debit	Credit
3	1	SI	28/07/2010	O/Bal inv	Opening Balance	342.98	0.00	342.98	
41	2	SI	02/08/2010	00300	Farm Collections x 8	175.20	0.00	175.20	
46	2	SI	04/08/2010	00302	Farm collections x 4	120.00 *	120.00	120.00	
48	1	SC	02/08/2010	55	Farm Collections x 2 (Broken)	16.80	0.00		16.80
58	1	SR	05/08/2010	BACS	Sales Receipt	342.98	0.00		342.98
74	1	SR	11/08/2010	BACS	Sales Receipt	158.40	0.00		158.40
						120.00	120.00	638.18	518.18

Amount Outstanding 120.00
Amount Paid this period 501.38
Credit Limit £ 8,000.00

A/C: PP002 **Name:** Perfect Pastimes Ltd **Contact:** Stan Hartley **Tel:** 07719 3612819

No	Items	Type	Date	Ref	Details	Value	O/S	Debit	Credit
2	1	SI	17/07/2010	O/Bal inv	Opening Balance	13,209.34 *	13,209.34	13,209.34	
						13,209.34	13,209.34	13,209.34	0.00

Amount Outstanding 13,209.34
Amount Paid this period 0.00
Credit Limit £ 15,000.00

A/C: PP004 **Name:** Prettypops Ltd **Contact:** Betty Chamberlain **Tel:** 0845 19828282

No	Items	Type	Date	Ref	Details	Value	O/S	Debit	Credit
4	1	SI	17/07/2010	O/Bal inv	Opening Balance	190.87	0.00	190.87	
61	1	SC	05/08/2010	BADDBT	Bad Debt Write Off	190.87	0.00		190.87
						0.00	0.00	190.87	190.87

Amount Outstanding 0.00
Amount Paid this period 0.00
Credit Limit £ 5,000.00

A/C: TW003 **Name:** Toyways plc **Contact:** Brian Mason **Tel:** 01872 62819203

No	Items	Type	Date	Ref	Details	Value	O/S	Debit	Credit
1	1	SI	15/07/2010	O/Bal inv 288	Opening Balance	1,235.76 *	0.00	1,235.76	
43	3	SI	02/08/2010	00301	Farm Collections x 5	150.00 *	150.00	150.00	
57	1	SR	03/08/2010	Cheque	Sales Receipt	1,235.76	0.00		1,235.76
71	1	SI	06/08/2010	00304	Pets collections x 30	324.00 *	324.00	324.00	
						474.00	474.00	1,709.76	1,235.76

Amount Outstanding 474.00
Amount Paid this period 1,235.76
Credit Limit £ 5,000.00

Task 4.5

(a)

Date:	02/07/2012			**Justin Timbercrafts**						Page:	1
Time:	10:38:41			**Aged Creditors Analysis (Summary)**							

Report Date:	02/07/2012	Supplier From:	
Include future transactions:	No	Supplier To:	ZZZZZZZZ
Exclude Later Payments:	No		

** NOTE: All report values are shown in Base Currency, unless otherwise indicated **

A/C	Name	Credit Limit	Turnover	Balance	Future	Current	Period 1	Period 2	Period 3	Older
GRT005	Grange Toys Ltd	£ 10,000.00	5,897.50	3,221.50	0.00	0.00	0.00	0.00	0.00	3,221.50
MCS003	Matchsticks Ltd	£ 5,000.00	3,343.26	1,680.00	0.00	0.00	0.00	0.00	0.00	1,680.00
WWW002	Willow Works Ltd	£ 8,500.00	528.29	288.00	0.00	0.00	0.00	0.00	0.00	288.00
		Totals:	9,769.05	5,189.50	0.00	0.00	0.00	0.00	0.00	5,189.50

(b)

Date:	20/07/2012			**Justin Timbercrafts**						Page:	1
Time:	15:34:07			**Aged Debtors Analysis (Summary)**							

Report Date:	20/07/2012	Customer From:	
Include future transactions:	No	Customer To:	ZZZZZZZZ
Exclude later payments:	No		

** NOTE: All report values are shown in Base Currency, unless otherwise indicated **

A/C	Name	Credit Limit	Turnover	Balance	Future	Current	Period 1	Period 2	Period 3	Older
FN001	Funnystuff Ltd	£ 1,000.00	80.00	96.00	0.00	0.00	0.00	0.00	0.00	96.00
HK006	Happykidz Ltd	£ 8,000.00	574.98	120.00	0.00	0.00	0.00	0.00	0.00	120.00
PP002	Perfect Pastimes Ltd	£ 15,000.00	13,209.34	13,209.34	0.00	0.00	0.00	0.00	0.00	13,209.34
TW003	Toyways plc	£ 5,000.00	1,630.76	474.00	0.00	0.00	0.00	0.00	0.00	474.00
		Totals:	15,495.08	13,899.34	0.00	0.00	0.00	0.00	0.00	13,899.34

Answer will depend on student choices

Task 4.6

Happykidz Ltd

Justin Timbercrafts			Justin Timbercrafts		
27 West Lane			27 West Lane		
Domley			Domley		
DN22 4RD			DN22 4RD		

	HK006			HK006	
Happykidz Ltd			Happykidz Ltd		
Churchill Shopping Centre			Churchill Shopping Centre		
	02/07/2012			02/07/2012	
Fearnley			Fearnley		
FN88 3DS	1		FN88 3DS	1	

NOTE: All values are shown in **Pound Sterling**			NOTE: All values are shown in	**Pound Sterling**	

28/07/10	O/Bal inv 0	Goods/Services	342.98		28/07/10	Goods/Services	342.98	
02/08/10	00300	Goods/Services	175.20		02/08/10	Goods/Services	175.20	
04/08/10	00302	Goods/Services	120.00 *		04/08/10	Goods/Services	120.00	
02/08/10	55	Credit		16.80	02/08/10	Credit		16.80
05/08/10	BACS	Payment		342.98	05/08/10	Payment		342.98
11/08/10	BACS	Payment		158.40	11/08/10	Payment		158.40

Perfect Pastimes Ltd

Perfect Pastimes Ltd
Hubley Industrial Estate

01/09/2010

Hubley

HB29 7FD

All values are shown in Pound Sterling

17/07/2010	00291	Goods/Services	£	13,209.34	£ 13,209.34

Task 4.7

01 September 2010

Perfect Pastimes Ltd
Hubley Industrial Estate

Hubley

HB29 7FD

Dear Stan Hartley

Your account with us is overdue. Please arrange for full and immediate settlement by first class mail.

Yours sincerely

Task 4.8

Answer will depend on student choices.

Task 4.9

(a)   Answer will depend on earlier entries by student.

Task 4.9

(b)

Date:	02/07/2012	**Justin Timbercrafts**		Page:	1
Time:	10:42:35	**Period Trial Balance**			

To Period: Month 12, June 2011

N/C	Name	Debit	Credit
0020	Equipment and Tools	2,330.00	
0030	Office Equipment	1,354.00	
0050	Motor Vehicles	4,586.00	
1100	Debtors Control Account	13,899.34	
1200	Bank Current Account		3,816.03
1230	Petty Cash	150.00	
2100	Creditors Control Account		5,189.50
2200	Sales Tax Control Account		171.49
2201	Purchase Tax Control Account	687.87	
3000	Capital		10,000.00
4000	Sales - Jungle Collection		17,428.50
4001	Sales - Farm Collection		19,364.70
4002	Sales - Pets Collection		10,692.45
4003	Cash Sales		5,581.85
4900	Miscellaneous Income		220.00
5000	Materials Purchased	31,604.80	
6201	Advertising	1,430.00	
7100	Rent and Rates	2,920.00	
7304	Miscellaneous Motor Expenses	9,805.51	
7400	Travelling	14.80	
7504	Office Stationery	2,399.33	
7801	Cleaning	20.00	
7901	Bank Charges	32.00	
8100	Bad Debt Write Off	190.87	
8200	Donations	200.00	
8204	Insurance	840.00	
	Totals:	72,464.52	72,464.52

INDEX